MUMM
THE STORY
OF A CHAMPAGNE HOUSE

Also by François Bonal:
Champagne, Lausanne, 1984.

François Bonal

MUMM
The Story of a Champagne House

ARTHAUD

Translated by Susan Allen and Doreen Broneer

I
THE STORY
OF A CHAMPAGNE HOUSE

1
The Beginnings of an Adventure

Rheims, 1 March, 1827. A certain G. Heuser entered into partnership with four Germans — three brothers, Jacobus, Gottlieb and Philipp Mumm, and Friedrich Giesler — to establish a firm there, called "P.A. Mumm and Co.," for the purpose of trading in the wines of Champagne.

What do we really know about these founders? Friedrich Giesler was from the Rhineland; that is the only information we have about his origins. Jacobus (1779-1835), Gottlieb (1782-1852) and Philipp (1782-1842) Mumm inherited a high-ranking social position from their father, Peter Arnold Mumm (1733-1797), whose family came from the Hesse district and had extensive vineyard holdings in the Rhine valley. In 1761, he had founded a wine business, the firm of "Peter Arnold Mumm," with headquarters in Cologne and a branch in Frankfurt: his three sons had later joined the business. These three brothers, the dynamic and strong-minded characters of the future P.A. Mumm and Co., therefore had the extensive commercial resources of Peter Arnold Mumm at their disposal.

Practically nothing is known of G. Heuser's past, or of his personality. That he had a well-established business in the main square of Rheims, with an international clientele for which the new company assumed responsibility, is clear from a brief note dated 12 September, 1827, to a broker in Marseille: *With respect to conditions of sale, we will continue to adopt the same ones which existed between yourself and our Mister Heuser.* From his correspondence, we learn that he was on good terms with the Parisian bankers, Rougemont of Lowenberg. Was he French perhaps? Was he a German who had established himself in later life in Rheims? In any event, he married a girl from Champagne: Madame Heuser led an active social life and visited suppliers. G. Heuser was the manager of, as well as a partner in, this new firm: he was authorised to sign on the company's behalf and reported his

activities to the remaining partners, who kept tight control of the Rheims company from Germany. The activities of the French and German companies overlapped for a long time. An entry discovered in the 1830 accounts of the Rheims company states that *42 bottles of white sparkling wine were sent to Frankfurt to be processed at the rate of 1.50 franc each.*

One may well wonder what drove Messieurs Mumm and Giesler to extend their interests into France. Personal motives, no doubt, but also the customs of the times. During the friendly peace which followed the Napoleonic wars, the western part of Germany and Champagne maintained good neighbour relations, notably in areas of trade. Attracted by the economic prosperity and cultural influence of France, young people came to Epernay, Ay, Avize and Rheims to train with champagne producers, and a certain percentage stayed to found their own Houses. Between 1820 and 1845 five of them became large wholesale champagne merchants, following the example of Florens-Louis Heidsieck, a native of the Hanover district, who had established her champagne House in Rheims in 1785.

The commercial success of sparkling wine from the end of the 17th century was incontestably among the reasons which motivated these Germans to choose the Champagne region for wine production. After a long period of trial and error, champagne came of age at the beginning of the 19th century: production increased tenfold in a few decades! From 300,000 bottles annually in the 1790's, it had climbed to three million bottles by the end of the 1820's, two thirds of which were exported. For wine merchants doing business in Germany, the temptation to come to France and share in this unexpected good fortune was strong — a temptation Messieurs Mumm and Giesler did not resist.

Production facilities and the necessary champagne making know-how,

◁◁ *J.-F. de Troy's,*
"The Oyster Lunch."
◁ *N. Lancret's,*
"The Ham Lunch."
(Courtesy of Lauros-Giraudon.)

as well as regular supplies of raw materials — grapes or still wines (non-sparkling) — were essential for business. At the outset, of course, the technical means of production were lacking. The firm was established at 14 rue de la Grosse-Bouteille (Big Bottle), name with a ring of destiny! Its premises next to the town hall were very likely those of M. Heuser. Although he was undeniably familiar with the techniques involved in champagne making, as certain of his letters show, M. Heuser was content at that time to work on the sales side of P. A. Mumm and Co. He traded in both still and sparkling white and rosé wine, as well as red wine, his main suppliers being Jacquinet-Jouron and Xavier Desbordes in Avize, Boileau-Guérin in Ay, and Labé in Rheims. These in turn bought from *top-rated localities* — Avize and Cramant, Ay and Mareuil, Sillery, Verzenay and Bouzy.

The "House," as the company was referred to, gave suppliers precise instructions for making the wines it purchased into champagne. It kept an eye on their development by requesting "trial batches," that is, samples of wine taken at different stages of vinification and second fermentation in bottle (*prise de mousse*), and then furnished the necessary products. Thus, on 27 November, 1827, M. Heuser wrote to Xavier Desbordes, promising to send him *12 cases of sugar-candy to "operate" on the wine we purchased from you,* "operation" being the term then used for *dosage* or sweetening. Fearing that Boileau-Guérin would not blend according to his instructions, on one occasion at least, he sent Madame Heuser along, requesting them to *organise themselves so they could start blending the 6 barrels as soon as she arrived.*

In December of the first trading year, the company wrote to Xavier Desbordes: *We beg you not to lose another instant in procuring the 40 barrels of wine from Cramant we directed you to buy on our behalf; we are more interested in quality than price, and wish to have only the very best.* A letter

▷ *Lurçat tapestry:*
The Seven Episode of the song of the World,
"Champagne."

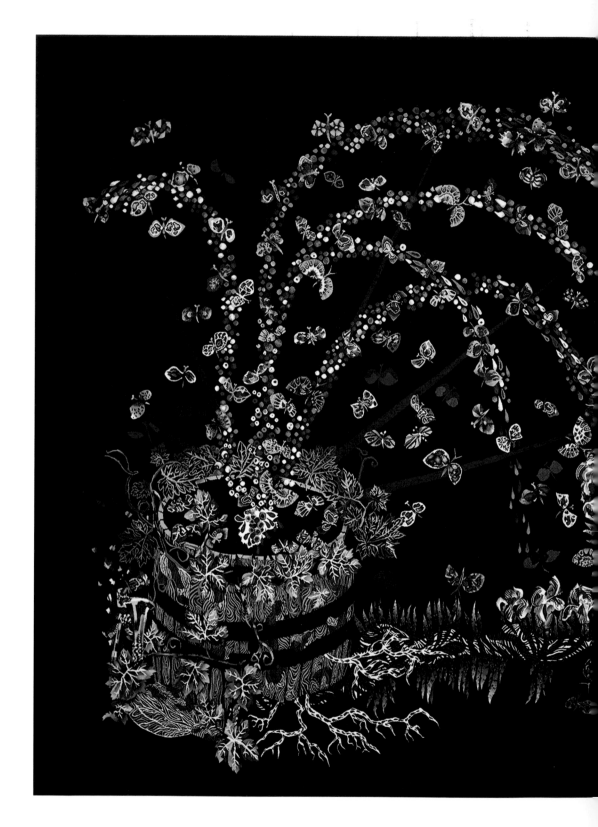

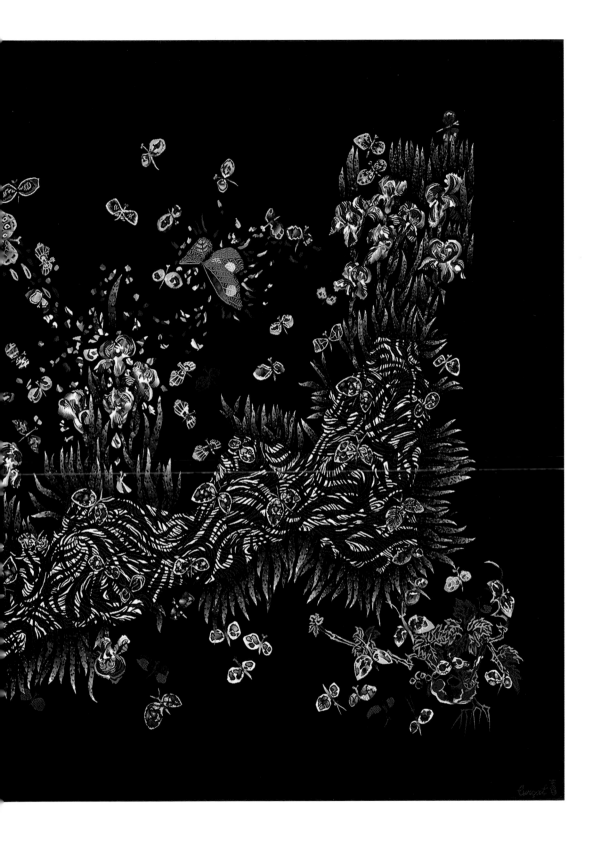

sent to Labé, asking him to *make 90 to 100 barrels of white wine from blends of Verzenay and Sillery*, included detailed instructions: *First of all contract to buy everything available for sale from the best vineyards, and we have decided, in order to obtain top quality wine, that grapes will be pressed only three times.* This confirms the concern for quality, hinted at previously, when wines from *top-rated localities* were being sought: this inviolable principle of the partners of 1827 and their successors still remains the pride of Mumm today.

The first sets of accounts made particular reference to still wines. Even Burgundy wines were mentioned, namely fifty bottles of Clos Vougeot 1822. This transaction must have been highly unusual however, because M. Heuser had to find out from a third party how to arrange their purchase. Sparkling wines, in other words champagne, were given due emphasis, the first consignments being shipped abroad on 17 March, 1827, a mere two weeks after the company opened its doors: 612 bottles to a merchant in Amsterdam and 350 bottles to the Hôtel de Russie in Leipzig. Most of the 1827 vintage was exported in fact, to the principal markets of Germany (36,000 bottles), Russia and Poland (18,000), Great Britain (7,000), the Netherlands (Holland and Belgium — 4,500), while only 771 bottles were sold in France. Mumm's export leanings were thus apparent from the very start.

A quick glance at the list of Mumm's early customers reveals that it supplied champagne to the highest echelons of international society. The Hôtel de Russie in Leipzig, mentioned above, was probably a luxury establishment. On 2 September, 1827, there is an order for a Baron de Rothschild, resident of Paris. Being a cautious financial man, he ordered only 6 bottles of champagne for a sum of 27.50 francs. One month later however, another

Rothschild, this one from Frankfurt, bought 50 bottles, quite likely influenced by his cousin's favourable opinion. Prince Ernst von Hessen Philippstahl, Prince Emil von Darmstadt, the Grand-Dukes Carl and Gustav von Mecklenburg-Schwerin and the courts of several other Grand-Dukes, plus fifteen or so German Counts and Barons, many of whom were generals or more senior still, are all listed in the 1827 accounts. So much for Germany. Consignments also appear for Lord Auckland in London, the Count of Wetterstedt, Minister of Foreign Affairs in Stockholm, Count Gourieff, the Russian ambassador in Brussells, the Duke of Looz, owner of a splendid Renaissance castle in Bentlage, near Bois-le-Duc, the Count of Baillet, Governor of West Flanders in Bruges, etc.

At the end of its first trading year, P.A. Mumm and Co. had sold 69,825 bottles of champagne to a first-rate clientele. This brilliant result meant its creation could only be hailed as a success.

Several factors came together to produce a rapid rise in the fortunes of the House of Mumm, soon enabling it to join the ranks of the greatest Champagne brand-names and conserve this privileged position until 1914. To begin with, it should be noted that the company became progressively concentrated into the hands of one of the branches of the Mumm family. M. Heuser disappeared from the firm shortly after 1830. M. Giesler left in 1837 to form his own company and market his own champagne, Giesler champagne, in Avize, a small market town of the Côte des Blancs, described by the wine merchant, Bertin de Rocheret, even in 1744 as being *quite large, its size having been considerably increased due to that insane invention, sparkling wine.*

On 13 June, 1838, in the presence of Monsieur Marguet, a Rheims lawyer, *an act with a view to forming a new company, in joint names, to do*

▷ *The Mumm Champagne family tree, 1827-1893.*
▷▷ *Jules Mumm Champagne created in 1852.*

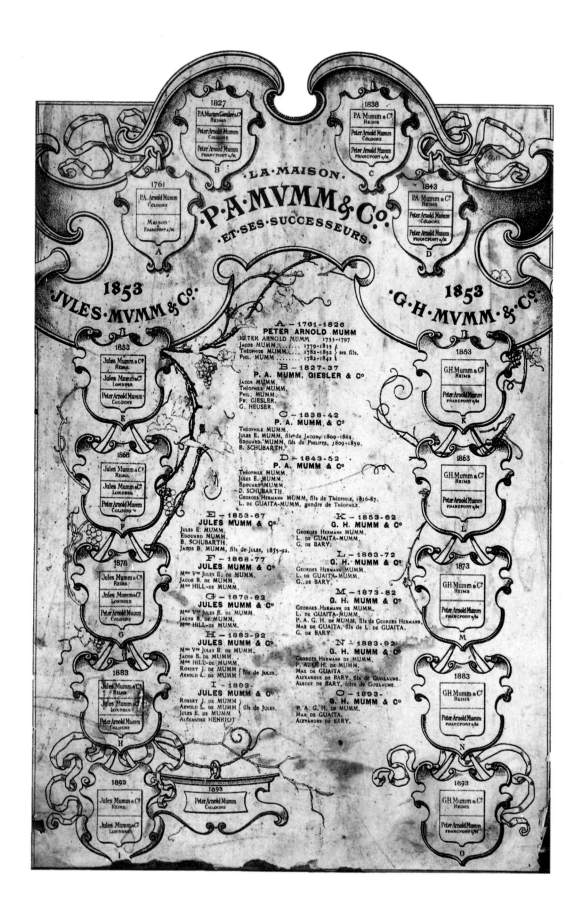

business in Champagne wines called "Pierre Arnaud Mumm and Co." was established. The partners were: *Mr Théophile Mumm, merchant, resident of Frankfurt; Mr Jules Mumm, wine merchant, resident of Cologne; Mr Edouard Frédéric Mumm, merchant, resident of Cologne; Mr Benoist Jacques Schubarth, resident of Rheims.* Théophile is French for Gottlieb, whom we have met already as one of the three founding brothers of Mumm. Jules (1809-1863), son of Jacobus, and Edouard Frédéric (1809-1859), son of Philipp, were his nephews. Nothing is known about Mr Schubarth, except that he already had shares in the company. The new company was run as a partnership: one partner stayed in France to look after the day to day running of the business, while the other three lived in Germany.

Things remained like this for twenty-four years. Théophile Mumm brought his son, Georges Hermann and his son-in-law, Leberecht von Guaïta, husband of his daughter, Mathilde, into the business; they both became partners in 1843. The firm splintered on Théophile's death probably as a result of differences between the partners, giving birth, in 1852, to two new companies, "Jules Mumm and Co." and "G.H. Mumm and Co." Some partners of the parent company took shares in the first, Jules and Edouard Frédéric Mumm and Benoist Jacques Schubarth joining Jacob Bernard Mumm (1835-1892), the son of Jules. The second company comprised Georges Hermann Mumm, who gave it his name, Leberecht von Guaïta, who added "Mumm" to his surname, and Guillaume de Bary, whose family was German despite its French-sounding name. Arriving in Rheims in 1837, he established himself there a short time later by working at "P.A. Mumm and Co.," where he eventually became managing director, a function he continued to exercise in the new company, his brother Albert acting as assistant manager.

After the split, each of these two Houses continued to maintain a very close relationship with the German firm of Peter Arnold Mumm, as P. A. Mumm and Co. had done. G.H. Mumm and Co., forged links with the Frankfurt office, where Messieurs Mumm and von Guaïta were on its board of directors; Jules Mumm and Co. established ties with the Cologne office. This latter firm ceases to be of interest at this point; it discontinued trading in 1903 and went into receivership in 1909-1910, at which time G.H. Mumm and Co. partly took it over.

The business continued its steady development until World War I, run by succeeding generations of partners, under the driving force of Georges Hermann von Mumm (the family has been ennobled in 1873). In 1912, P.A.M.H. von Mumm became head of the company. His mother and brother Walther, as well as Léon von Guaïta, one of Max's sons, also held shares.

G.H. Mumm and Co. had operated autonomously since the 1850's, even though links with the family companies in Germany had been maintained. In 1886 it had initiated the foundation of the Association of Champagne Merchants with Albert de Bary as vice-president. On his death, Alexandre de Bary was elected to the special committee and given responsibility for preparing Champagne's participation in the 1900 World Fair.

The Mumm, Guaïta and Bary families started to take part in the social life of Rheims from around this time: they were invited out, and they, in turn, received guests. Gottlieb von Mumm, Georges Hermann's son, continued to live in Frankfurt but his children lived in Rheims; Walther at 7 rue de la Justice, Hermann and Sigmund at 17 Boulevard Lundy, where Alex-

▷ Vallée de la Marne
vineyards.

andre de Bary lived as well. Sigmund, a retired horseman, would go riding at first light of dawn on the grounds of the Champ de Mars; the success of his horses on racecourses throughout France earned him a national reputation. Alexandre de Bary ("de" being the equivalent of "von") was president of the Rheims regattas. Marriages were arranged with Champagne families and children were born in Rheims itself. Raoul de Bary, Albert's son, married a Miss Goulet, entitling him to a seat on the board of directors of the champagne House, Georges Goulet.

How did Mumm produce sparkling wines before 1914? Although at first non-sparkling reds, rosés and whites accounted for the major portion of the company's business, this sector of activity was rapidly abandoned, in order to devote attention exclusively to the sparkling wines of Champagne, in other words, champagne. P.A. Mumm and Co. bought in the first instance from the small producers who had supplied M. Heuser's business. With efficiency and quality considerations uppermost, the firm made a huge effort to organise its own sparkling wine production as quickly as possible. This was not easy, for it meant ensuring a regular grape supply, and acquiring the production facilities, equipment and know-how.

Mumm owned no vines for half a century, apart from a patch in Verzenay, purchased in 1840 and reduced in 1880 to 0.23 hectares: it covered all its raw material needs by buying in grapes and wine. Vineyard maintenance was such a hazardous business that many champagne Houses preferred to leave the risks involved to the growers who owned the land.

In that era, and even right up to World War I, champagne vines were grown *en foule*, that is, crowded on top of each other. To begin with, planting was actually done in either regular or staggered rows, but then two processes were carried out which gradually destroyed this beautifully ordered arrangement — *provignage* (layering) and *assiselage* (burying). The object of the first was to fill in a gap where a vine was missing, or to increase the overall number of vines in a given area. It was done by burying a cane so it would take root and produce a new vine. *Assiselage*, unlike layering, was done every year, and consisted of flattening vines on the ground after having separated them from each other by about twenty centimetres, then covering them with soil, leaving only one cane protruding. This formed a large tangled mass of young rootlets going in every direction, in fresh, rich new earth, and aerated the soil at the same time. Vine density went as high as 50,000 vines per hectare, six times that of today.

Vines then, however, were not supported by wire trellises as they are now. Instead, each Spring a process called *la ficherie* had to be carried out, a time-consuming and fastidious operation, which consisted of driving a wooden stake into the ground beside each vine to serve as a support, then attaching the vine to it. This was done by hand, with or without the help of a mallet; or to assist pushing the stake well down, a type of metal plate was fitted to the worker's shoe or his chest protected by a *planchot*, a wooden breast-plate covered with leather. After the harvest, the vine props had to be pulled up, put into a pile, and sharpened and disinfected during winter. To all this work, specific to vines planted *en foule*, had to be added the maintenance tasks required by every vineyard — principally ploughing, weeding, pruning, tying up canes, grubbing out excess buds, and pulling off superfluous vegetation, forcing sap to be concentrated in the productive part of the vine. In addition, new vines had to be planted, and soil reconstituted during winter by adding topsoil and spreading fertiliser. Vines were too tightly bunched together for horses, or even wheelbarrows, to penetrate, with the result that all work was carried out by hand and all carrying done on mens' backs.

Growing vines *en foule* was arduous for the grower; one old timer described this harsh era, saying: *We squirmed about like snakes in those vineyards.*

Uncertainty of the results only added to growers' distress. The existence of natural disasters, diseases and parasites which threatened vines meant living in a state of perpetual anxiety. Hurricanes, rainstorms which washed soil away and formed gullies in the narrow tracks, hail which chopped up leaves and destroyed young shoots, Spring frosts capable of annihilating an entire harvest in a few moments, were all awaited with dread. Growers also feared the harsh, though less frequent, winter frosts.

Waiting for flowering during the latter half of June, and sometimes into July, was disquieting. If it took place rapidly, healthy and well-proportioned grapes were formed, but more often than not it dragged on. If fertilisation was poor and ovaries left unpollinated, the number of grapes was reduced, a condition known as *coulure*. The result of a long, drawn out flowering, was *millerandage,* or dwarf-sized berries, sometimes in large numbers: if it was late as well, then vintage could be delayed and, as a consequence, more exposed to frost and rot. Henri Soullié, a substantial vineyard owner, grower and broker in Cumières, made a note in his diary on this subject: *1879 was a disastrous year. Flowering had scarcely finished by 25 July and grapes had suffered "coulure." Vintage did not start until 12 October and the 17th, a severe frost stripped the vines of all their leaves. Very little wine and of poor quality.*

Not to mention "enemy invaders" and vine diseases! At times considerable damage was caused by insects, such as the pyrale moth, particularly active between 1835 and 1840. The cochylis moth, known as the "mischievous-worm," was also dreaded, as was the leaf-curl moth, also called the "cigar-roller" because it caused leaves to roll up in the shape of a cigar.

Another unwelcome visitor was a small black beetle called "the writer" because its manner of eating vine leaves made them look as if someone had written on them. Insects were not the only menace, there were rodents as well — field voles, for example, laid waste Champagne's vines in 1873. Starlings, then as now, were a common sight around vineyards.

In those times, there was nothing with which to combat these scourges, so growers relied on time-honoured measures, such as those recommended at the beginning of the 18th century in the *Treatise on Vinegrowing in Champagne* by Brother Pierre, Benedictine monk at the Abbey of Haut-villers, for example: *And if leaf-curl moths, which are harmful to vines, should appear in the vineyard, their skins should be removed and put into bags, which should be burned some distance from the vines, then the ashes buried.*

Vineyards suffered exceptionally severe attacks of fungal disease in the 19th century. Grey rot raged unchecked, and powdery mildew, which could fortunately be controlled by sulphur spraying, appeared from the 1850's. Vines had to be "treated" ten to fifteen times per year, and it is not difficult to imagine how exhausting it was for growers to trudge through the vineyards for six straight weeks in wet summers, sprayers on their backs, "without even enough time to take off their braces."

So owning vines in the middle of the 19th century was a constant headache. Henri Soullié wrote in his notes: *My vines need another sulphur-ing, damn it!* and further on: *Vines are a poor investment for a man with a family to support.* This explains the reticence of champagne Houses to set up vineyards for themselves, most preferring to leave such risks to vineyard owners and instead buy their wines where, in any case, they virtually stipulated the asking price, depending on their needs and the abundance of

△ *Work in the Marne vineyards in 1913.*

supplies. Growers, therefore, dreaded very heavy crops. In 1854, Henri Soullié observed: *The wine is very good, but because of the extent of coulure, the likes of which has never been witnessed in living memory, the most productive vineyards yielded little more than 150 to 200 litres per hectare. Unprecedented prices are being asked as a consequence, exceeding 300 francs for two hectos of Cumières and over 500 francs for Verzenay and Bouzy. This makes it the fifth year there has been a tiny harvest of mediocre quality. Such scarcity has been a blessing in disguise in a way, because it has meant an end to the disastrous prices of 1847 to 1850.* Twenty-five years later, he even went so far as to say: *Very little wine and of mediocre quality, which despite that, is selling at insane prices because demand from the trade is so high.* In fact, champagne Houses made the laws to their own advantage, because if the harvest was big and they had plenty of stock they didn't buy at all, or paid ridiculously low prices.

From the end of the 1850's however, it became usual for *grands crus* (top vineyards) to sell grapes rather than wine, a practice imposed by merchants who found it served their interests; a perishable commodity is easier to buy at a good price than a ready-made product capable of being stored for future speculation. Champagne Houses were thus able to choose their grapes on the basis of quality, and demand that bunches be sorted during vintage: entire bunches could be rejected, or those parts which were spoiled or insufficiently ripe, cut off and thrown away. These procedures, ignored in other French wine producing regions, were carried out on long, narrow wicker trays, called *clayettes,* which were put down at the end of the vineyard on *manne-quins* — wicker-baskets used for harvesting, with a capacity of 60 to 100 kilos of grapes, depending on the district. Purchasing grapes also meant that Mumm could press the grapes it bought itself, at least all those from the north face of the Montagne de Reims, using the presses installed at Verzenay in 1843. For its own grapes, as well as those pressed by growers' on its behalf under its watchful eye, it could therefore ensure correct division of the must into one *cuvée,* or vat, of the very finest quality, and *tailles* of lesser quality, conforming to a Champagne tradition originating at the beginning of the 18th century. A manual written in that era explained that, to obtain the latter, *the outside edges of the grape mass are firmly and squarely trimmed using a large shovel with a cutting edge, and everything cut from the sides specifically rejected; for this reason the remaining grape mass is called the "taille," or that which has been trimmed.* Buying grapes, moreover, was the only way which enabled the company's own cellarmaster to control vinification completely, and thus guarantee the quality of the wine.

In 1882, the company bought 7.6 hectares in the village of Cramant in the Côte des Blancs. Why this sudden change? Perhaps it was due to Alexandre de Bary's appointment that year to the company's board of directors, although the vines were bought in the name of the Mumm family. Being a good manager, he was probably aiming to diversify the House's sources of grape supply in a period when champagne sales were booming: at the same time, it meant greater independence with respect to grape suppliers.

G.H. Mumm and Co. however, limited its acquisition to 8 hectares. Vineyard land was expensive because champagne sold well, and since the company decided to buy in the best localities, it was obliged to pay up to 40,000 francs per hectare when the price of lesser quality vineyards was only 8,000 francs. Furthermore, available land for sale had to be found, and competition was keen between champagne Houses. Apart from that, establishing vineyards was a long, drawn-out operation, and their maintenance required knowledge which took many years to acquire. Downy mildew, the

dreaded fungal disease which had appeared in 1882, invaded the entire champagne vineyard region again in 1886, causing considerable damage.

In the end, Mumm did not resume setting up its own vineyards until 1906. First of all, it extended its holdings in the Côte des Blancs that same year by buying 4.79 hectares in Avize, then 7.65 at Oiry in 1913, supplemented by a further 2.57 hectares in 1914: it increased its vineyard area in Cramant from 8 to 22 hectares. Mumm diversified by buying 12 hectares, mostly in Ay, with the remainder spread throughout Mareuil-sur-Ay, Dizy, in the Vallée de la Marne, and Avenay and Mutigny in the Vallée de la Livre, a tributary of the Marne.

In 1914, the company owned around 50 hectares in all, 37 in the Côte des Blancs, white grape territory, the rest in the Montagne de Reims and the Vallée de la Marne, which supplied it with black grapes. These latter, Pinot Noir, were called "Morillon Noir" in the 16th century and, in those days, in conjunction with "Fromenteau," were responsible for the success of Champagne wine: today "Fromenteau" (Pinot Gris) exists only in Alsace, where it is made into Tokay. With respect to white grapes, the more ancient varieties of mediocre quality had consistently been replaced from the middle of the 18th century in the Côte des Blancs by Chardonnay, a variety related to Pinot Blanc with a long-standing reputation for yielding the best white grapes in Burgundy and Champagne.

Hand-in-hand with the constitution of its own vineyards, Mumm equipped itself with the necessary means to transform its own vintage into must. Even before it had bought its first vines, it had set up presses in Verzenay for pressing grapes bought from other vineyard owners. These were housed in a *vendangeoir* or press-house, the term in Champagne given to the building designed to provide shelter for presses and lodge the grape

△ *Wicker* mannequin,
a large wine-harvest basket.

pickers. The British writer Vizetelly visited the Verzenay press-house in the 1870's: *G.H. Mumm and Co. have a large press-house at Verzenay containing four presses; three driven by broad hand-wheels, needing several men to turn them, the fourth equipped with a screw turned by means of a long rod. The 3,600 kilos of grapes put into each press yields ten barrels for sparkling wine production and, in addition, three to four barrels of inferior wine for consumption by the workers. Pressing starts at 6 in the morning and continues until midnight.* This provides an illustration of the principle in Champagne known as "fractionation" of the must, which decrees that wine obtained at the end of pressing, following the prolonged crushing of grapes, has little to recommend it, and must not be used to make champagne. This will be discussed in greater detail later.

The company progressively equipped itself with other press-houses, close to its main sources of grapes — its own vines or those of its regular suppliers. In 1914, it owned vineyards at Verzenay and Verzy, in the Montagne de Reims, at Ay, in the Vallée de la Marne, at Avize, and at Cramant, in the Côte des Blancs. The press-houses in these areas were equipped respectively with five, four, two, five and two presses: a total of eighteen.

In the same period, the company recruited growers to work their vineyards and others to manage them. To encourage them to stay with the company, pensions and retirement plans, assistance during periods of military service, plus paid holidays, childbirth and family death allowances were introduced. A "Friendly Association of Workers of the House of G.H. Mumm and Co." was set up and run with the company's encouragement and assistance. Exactly the same social benefits applied to cellar workers, such initiatives being remarkably ahead of their time.

By the eve of World War I, the company had really become what is called in Champagne, a "vineyard-oriented House." Its viticultural domaine extended throughout the most prestigious vineyard areas, particularly Ay, Avize and Cramant, these "top-rated localities" from which P.A. Mumm and Co. strove to procure grapes and wine as far back as 1827. Its own vineyards were still insufficient to cover all its needs but, due to its network of press-houses, it could exercise control over the pressing of a large part of the additional grapes bought from its usual suppliers in the top-rated areas. Mumm, therefore, could not have been in a better position to produce excellent champagne. The company steadily increased its production capacity until 1914, constantly making sure that grape supply kept up with demand. The original buildings used for M. Heuser's business on the rue de Mars were rapidly outgrown; they were ill-adapted as well, and therefore modified up to the time of the company split, which resulted in the two firms of G.H. Mumm and Co. and Jules Mumm and Co. The latter kept these premises, which it later extended up to No. 6 rue de Mars.

G.H. Mumm and Co. took advantage of the situation to expand its premises and, in a memorandum dated 1st January, 1853, advised its customers that it had *built entirely new cellars and premises suited in every way to the current demands of the Champagne wine business.* The new facilities formed a large harmonious unit in the Rue Coquebert neighbourhood, with the main entrance at 24 rue Andrieux, and a side entrance at 17 Boulevard du Temple (now Boulevard Lundy). The cellars dug out there, manually of course, at that time, did not need supports to hold them up. In both summer and winter, the temperature fluctuated between 9° C and is maintained around 11° C. Before the arrival of electricity, the cellars were lit by means of wrought iron "cellar lamps," composed of a tripod and sliding apparatus for the candle, which could then be adjusted to the height required. In the next phase, the cellars were equipped with two parallel electric wires straddled by a light, sliding wooden slat with a copper band at either end for receiving the current. In the middle of the slat, a flexible wire connected to a bulb provided an ingenious form of mobile lighting. Bottles were placed in baskets hooked onto continuous chains to lower them down to the cellar.

G.H. Mumm had henceforth excellent cellars at its disposal, with storerooms of vast proportions above them. However, judging this capacity too small to meet the company's needs, it rented space at 35 and 37 rue Coquebert. This transfer marked an important step in Mumm's development; it thereby acquired a position in a new neighbourhood already occupied by several highly regarded champagne merchants. There are numerous references to it in the written works of the period. A *Travellers' Guide* of 1883, relates that *these gentlemen have surrounded their storerooms with handsome facades* and that *from 1852, several export Houses, notably Messieurs G. H. Mumm and L. Roederer, have had extensive facilities built on the site of the former ramparts, having excavated and cut regular, multiple cellars out of the chalk deposits of the Coquebert neighbourhood — a very peculiar sight to visitors.*

In 1880, the company extended its estate once again, raising the storerooms and excavating cellars in the rue du Champ-de-Mars. The whole operation was repeated after buying land situated between rue Gosset and rue du Champ-de-Mars. In 1899, on the death of Alexandre du Bary, the company proceeded to purchase the private hotel at 31 rue du Champ-de-Mars, finally abandoning rue Andrieux and Boulevard Lundy for new premises. From 1907, the company's registered headquarters and offices were located at number 34, and moved in 1913 to number 29 of the same street.

Reconstitution
of an antique press.

2

The Production of a Great Wine

To make Champagne wine sparkling was not an easy task in the first part of the 19th century. Things were still at the empirical stage, fermentation being an eternal source of frustration. The making of a commodity whose method of production was so full of hazards was only justified by the privileged classes' infatuation with champagne, and their willingness to pay high prices to get it.

These days, the starting point for making champagne is "still" wine, which results from the biological fermentation of the sugar in grape juice the "must," obtained by the action of yeasts (fermentation agents) found on the film of the grapeskin. This fermentation ("vinification") produces both alcohol and carbon dioxide gas, which is allowed to escape spontaneously. In order to become champagne, the wine must undergo another fermentation, this time in a hermetically sealed bottle. More sugar and yeasts must be added to recreate the conditions of primary fermentation since the initial supply has been exhausted. More alcohol and carbon dioxide is formed, but it remains imprisoned, forming the froth when the bottle is opened. The amount of sugar added is calculated in order to achieve the desired pressure, (6 atmospheres for standard champagne), at the end of fermentation.

In the 19th century, storeroom temperatures were subject to the whims of nature. Vinifications were incomplete and, since it was not known how to calculate the amount of residual sugar, the amount needed to bring about the desired pressure was unknown. Until the 1880's, nothing was known of the role of yeasts. Practicality was the order of the day for many years; its consequences known as "breakages": cellars were full of exploding bottles as excess pressure shattered glass which was moreover, less solid than it is today. In the 18th century, up to 90 % of bottles delivered to the cellar could end up broken. In 1840, the average was 20 %; in 1880, an 8 % breakage rate was considered normal. Wine lost in the massacre was recovered from the drains and used to make vinegar. Tourists visiting the cellars were even made to wear fencing masks as a safety measure! *The noise of exploding bottles here and there*, recounted Vizetelly, *is deafening and, while the echo gets fainter, it is mixed with the tinkling sound of escaping wine as it cascades to the bottom of the stack and trickles down the inclined floor to the narrow central drain.*

The anxiety which reigned at Mumm, as indeed everywhere during second fermentation, can be imagined, even if the bottles were the best to be had in the region, or even in northern France. About a dozen suppliers were listed in the accounts of 1907, Charbonneaux of Rheims, the Glassmakers of Neuvillette Pty Ltd, Bergerlord and Co. of Anor and the Glassmakers of Hirson being the three major ones. Orders appeared for 80 cl bottles, (called *champenoise)*, magnums (two bottles), pints (half-bottles) and half-pints (quarter bottles). Bottles were washed before use, Vizetelly describing the best method: *insert a certain number of glass beads in bottles filled with water; these replace the lead shot used in other Houses which has the disadvantage of leaving lead particles sticking to the inner surface of bottles.*

Before bottling, or *tirage*, different wines from diverse areas and years were blended. The object of this operation, called *assemblage*, was to create a *cuvée* or blend which was, as described in a handbook of the period, *a harmonious and homogenous whole, where different bouquets combined with, improved and complimented each other.* Champagne is the only region *assemblage* takes place; it is, however, indispensable in northern areas where weather is unpredictable and harvests very irregular. In the 19th century, since no one knew how to protect effectively against vine diseases, crops were often deplorable or even disastrous. For example, one vineyard owner's notebook contained the following appraisals: *1850-1851, poor quality; 1852, mediocre quality; 1853, average quality*, and it was not until 1856 before *good quality* finally appeared! Producers thus kept a reasonable quantity of "reserve wines" of acceptable quality for improving, or sometimes replacing, the current year's wines. Mumm always had large stocks of top quality reserve wines at its disposal, in spite of the financial burden it imposed.

Assemblage was absolutely necessary in Champagne for another reason: the vineyard area was very piecemeal, as the oenologist, Robert, reported in his *General Wine Handbook* in 1877: *because estates there are infinitely divided up, merchants have to blend wines from a great number of vineyard owners.* This was used to advantage by balancing, in the light of knowledge and experience, a variety of vineyards, so certain wines could make up for qualities lacking in others. This was what Horace was complaining of not being able to do, when he wrote: *I have neither vines in Falerne, nor on the slopes of Formie, to correct the wine of my own vineyard by judicious blending.*

All *assemblages* to determine the *cuvée* took place in a laboratory, and included — tasting glass in one hand and pen in the other — the cellarmaster and his assistants, but also, according to Champagne tradition, the owners, Messieurs de Mumm, de Bary and de Guaïta. Because champagne was principally a brand-name wine, the *cuvée* allowed the House to remain faithful to its style which, whenever necessary, was modified imperceptibly over several years. It also served the purpose of adapting its wine to the taste of foreign consumers.

Once the proportions of the various wines to be blended were determined, they were extracted and mixed in large casks. Vizetelly explained that these *were placed side by side and linked by hosepipes to a pair of small tanks, each with about half a dozen taps with syphons attached, thus permitting this same number of bottles to be filled simultaneously*. Mumm employed extra temporary staff to wash and carry bottles for this operation, called tirage.

Particular care was taken when sealing with corks, as recommended by Canon Godinot as far back as 1719: *One cannot be too careful in selecting good corks, wine does not spoil in certain containers because the container itself is faulty*. Cork was brought in from Catalonia and Andalucia and moulded in Champagne; from the 1850's to the present day, Mumm has bought its corks from the firm of Clignet. Fitting the neck of a bottle with a piece of cork twice its diameter was not an easy operation. In 1843 it was described thus: *It was not so long ago when coopers knew no other method for flattening a cork and forcing it into the neck of a bottle than to grip it between their teeth, which was bad for certain people's health and, in every case, very tiring and not terribly suitable*. The first corking machine appeared the same year as P.A. Mumm and Co. was founded. Although it was far from ideal, it wasn't long before the company could put it into operation, taking advantage of improvements as they came along. It was replaced in the 1860's by a much more satisfactory drop-hammer machine, developed by a M. Charbonnier of Epernay, consisting of a sliding head running between two vertical grooves. The idea was given to him, according to the *Vigneron Champenois* of 1899, by one of his apprentices who had watched the guillotine in operation in one of the town squares. This machine was later improved by a combination of mallet and sliding head but, just before the war, Mumm began to install electric corking machines working on the Lemaire system.

Corking was followed by *ficelage* or tying down. In order to prevent any untimely popping of the cork, the *ficeleur* attached it to the ring of the bottle neck with two oily pieces of string in the shape of a cross. Since there were two pieces of string, he had to do this process twice for each bottle, at

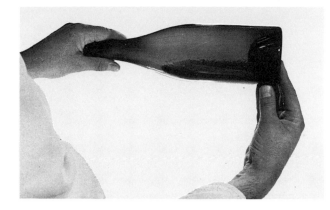

the rate of 1,000 to 1,200 bottles per day! Nicaise's "mechanical tying machine" however, also adopted by Mumm, made the operation easier from around 1870. The company later replaced string with wire muzzles which were affixed mechanically. According to Vizetelly, a team of 8 people could then put corks in and wire muzzles on 35 to 40,000 bottles per day.

Champagne making had one other special feature comprising two steps — *remuage* and *dégorgement* — in order to get rid of the sediment formed by yeasts during secondary fermentation. André Jullien described both operations in his *Wine Waiter's Handbook* of 1813: *A bottle was held by the neck, horizontally to begin with, and vibrated on its own axis till the deposit came away and collected in a single mass in the middle of the lower cavity; the same movement was continued with the bottle at an angle, in order to coax the deposit towards the neck. It was then placed in one of the holes of a bottle-rack maintaining this same angle. This standard procedure was carried out on a hundred bottles. When the rack was full, the first bottle was taken again, vibrated again tilting it even further, and put back in the rack at the more inclined angle. After vibrating the rest of the bottles in the same fashion, they were taken out a third time and shaken again; on this last manipulation the deposit had to be in the neck of the bottle, which was now placed in the rack in a completely upside down position. The wine was left to rest like that for several days till the deposit was well and truly cohesive and stuck to the cork. The cork was then released with the bottle in that same position, the deposit being forced out with the wine.*

This system of taking bottles from the rack one by one and putting them back every time the deposit needed shaking down was terribly time-consuming. The trade was dismayed; the requirements of business demanded a faster method. It was suggested therefore that bottles be left in their racks during

△ *"A bottle was held by the neck..."*

the entire *remuage* period, holes being cut obliquely in order to vary the angle of inclination. Although this represented considerable progress, it was greatly improved by the invention of the *pupitre de remuage* — two wooden racks hinged together in the form of an upside-down V, holding a total of 120 bottles. This gained not only space, but especially time, because cellar workers could work standing up and have equal access to every row. At the end of the 19th century they were very skilfully turning, shaking and vibrating up to 30,000 bottles per day.

The technique of *remuage* now being satisfactory, there remained the problem of irregularly formed deposits, and it was sometimes difficult, if not impossible, to collect them in the neck of the bottle for disgorging: sometimes they adhered strongly to the side of the bottle, forming *masques* (masks) — one continuous curve, or *griffes* (claws) — shaped like a dwarf palm tree, fold upon fold fanning out from a point in the bottle neck. To remedy this drawback, bottles were hit gently several times with a hammer, or struck vigorously on a wooden surface. The knack of well-executed disgorging varied with individual cellar workers but, no matter how experienced they were, quite a large amount of wine was still lost.

Champagne was considered a dessert wine in the 19th century, as proved in the *Song-book of Champagne Wine*, dating from 1890:

Champagne comes with dessert
In dusty bottles decorated with silver paper
Its company bringing us cheer
Sweet resolutions and joyous refrains

Sweetening had to be added since secondary fermentation had entirely stripped the wine of its sugar. This technique was known today as the *dosage*. The small quantity of wine lost during *dégorgement* was replaced by *liqueur d'expédition*, a sugar and wine mixture. The procedure was difficult because froth formed, and it was not until 1844 that a fairly crude machine was invented to do the job. Maumené described the *liqueur* in his *Theoretical and Practical Manual on Winemaking Operations*, published in 1873: *Theoretically the liqueur is a solution of pure sugar and wine, but in practice is much more complex than that, because it is adjusted to accommodate consumer preferences.* He listed the ingredients normally found in a *liqueur* for the English market: *sugar, water, champagne from the cuvée, port, cognac essence, Fismes dye, kirsch, rasberry brandy, and saturated solutions of alum, tartaric acid and tannin.* It is obvious that champagne had close ties with chemistry at that time. Customers however received soothing reassurances from producers who, with no concern at all for people's health, referred to a report of the great chemist Chaptal and declared that *Fismes dye in particular, was nothing more than a fruit extract with extra colouring matter.*

Once *dosage* had taken place, the final corking was carried out using similar techniques to the initial one. Yet, according to Vizetelly, *at Messieurs G.H. Mumm and Co., champagne destined for export had the exposed surface of their corks dipped in a kind of varnish to protect it against insects, and prevent the string going mouldy for several years. In humid weather, when the varnish took a long time to dry, the necks of bottles were placed facing downwards to allow the excess to run off. Corks were then heated gently on a drying rack with a 500 bottle capacity.*

Over the years, Mumm set up its own laboratories, enabling it to participate in research concerning the control of secondary fermentation.

▷ *Vines in winter.*
▷▷ *Flowering of the vine at the end of spring.*

G H MUMM & C°
REIMS
PETER ARNOLD MUMM
FRANKFURT °/M

Invoice of Champagne to be shipped from Antwerp to Philadelphia and consigned for sale for account and risk of whom it may concern:

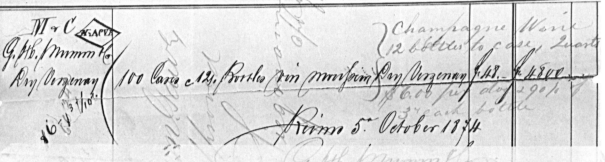

M & C
G. H. Mumm & C°
Roy Vergenay

100 Cases c 12 Bottles *vin mousseux Roy Vergenay* fr 48. fr 4800

Reims 5. October 1874

Champagne Wine
12 bottles to case, Quarts

$6.00 per doz = 90 &
3° each bottle

$6.

United States Consulate, Reims, France.

Je soussigné déclare que je suis *Gérant de Messr G. H. Mumm & C° Expéditeur* des denrées, produits et marchandises désignés dans la facture maintenant produite et ci-annexée; que ladite facture est vraie et loyale à tous égards; qu'elle contient un compte plein et fidèle du véritable prix courant desdits denrées, produits et marchandises au temps et au lieu où les mêmes ont été acquis ou fabriqués; que ladite facture ne contient que les escomptes, primes et décomptes réellement alloués, et qu'aucune autre facture desdits denrées, produits et marchandises n'a été et ne sera fournie à qui que ce soit. Je déclare en outre que lesdits denrées, produits et marchandises sont en destination du port de *Philadelphia* aux Etats-Unis d'Amérique.

Albert de Bary

I, **Adolph Gouverneur Gill,** United States Consul at Reims, France, do hereby certify that the within Invoice numbered _454_, in which are mentioned and described certain Goods, Wares and Merchandise, amounting, with the charges thereon, to the gross sum of _4800._ frcs. was produced to me by the subscriber of the foregoing who thereupon declared that it was intended to make entry of said Goods, Wares and Merchandise at the Port above named. I do further certify that I am satisfied that the person making the declaration hereto annexed is the person he represents himself to be; that he is a credible person and that so far as I have the means of knowing, the statements made in the said declaration are true

Witness my hand and the Consular Seal this _7th_ day of _Oct_ 1874

Received $ 2.50.

(Signed in triplicate.)

Adve Gouverneur Gill

United States Consul

Goods, Wares, and Merchandise have not been purchased.

François, a pharmacist from Châlons, pioneered this research shortly after 1830, attempting to determine the rational usage of sugar and yeasts. Robinet and Maumené followed in his footsteps in the 1870's. There was no tangible progress until the 20th century, but champagne making techniques nevertheless improved slowly from the middle of the 19th century.

In his book, *Champagne, The Wine, The Land and The People*, Patrick Forbes notes that in 1836 Mumm imported some enormous 12,000 litre casks from the Palatinate for carrying out the first fermentation, in order to give their wines a more uniform character than had been possible with smaller casks. He adds that the idea was soon taken up by other firms. Company technicians invented and perfected "wine machines," "bottle-shatterers" and other systems, as ingenious as they were hazardous, to check bottle strength.

Facilities for "*dégorgement* by freezing" were installed to increase efficiency. This process, dating from 1884, meant that bottles were maintained in the final position of *remuage*, that is face-downwards, then their necks plunged for fifteen to twenty minutes into a *refrigerated tank designed for bottle necks* filled with brine at −20°C. With *dégorgement*, the frozen liquid in the bottle neck shot out as a block of ice with the sediment imprisoned inside. This method diminished wine losses and avoided dispersal of the sediment at the same time.

▷ *Pinot flowers and bunches.*
▷▷ *Chardonnay.*

3

The Years of Achievement

From 1827 to 1914, Mumm released wine whose characteristics reflected this evolution in champagne making techniques. In 1880, and even up to 1914, although quality was not as consistent as it is today, its wines throughout the range were amongst the finest produced in Champagne.

From the beginning, degrees of pressure were specified; *grand mousseux, mousseux, demi-mousseux* and *tisane de Champagne*, in descending order. *Grand mousseux* was in greatest demand because, at the time, it was common to pop corks, and it gushed in a column right up to the ceiling. In 1840, however, its pressure was barely 2 atmospheres, and it wasn't until 1875 that it reached 5 to 6 atmospheres. *Mousseux* was slightly lower in pressure and, generally, quality. *Demi-mousseux* had very little pressure. Connoisseurs appreciated it (and still do) under the name *crémant. Less sparkling in the glass, (its) froth forms a sheet of foam covering the liquid which dissipates in a few moments; (its) advantage over "grand mousseux" wines is its stronger vinous quality.*

Rosé champagne, which Mumm shipped from the very first days of the company's existence, was prepared during *assemblage*, just prior to bottling. On 27 July, 1827, Mumm took delivery of 206 bottles of sparkling rosé from Jacquinet-Jouron in Avize. A short time later, M. Heuser wrote to one of his customers: *Rosé is in no way inferior to white wine. It is a real ladies' wine, and we wanted to pay special attention to their needs.* In this period, *œil-de-perdrix* (partridge's eye) and rosé were used interchangeably, but the latter rapidly became the more common term. Good rosé champagne is always made by a rapid fermentation of black grapes, or by mixing red and white Champagne wine but, in the first half of the 19th century, it was common to produce it by colouring white wine with Fismes dye, previously mentioned as a component of the *liqueur de tirage.*

Finally, during *assemblage*, "vintage" champagnes, a term which did not exist in the 19th century, were blended. Generally they were only ever made up in *grand mousseux*, and produced from wines of a single year, but there were no regulations at the time so, at very best, they existed in modest proportions. In *The History of Champagne*, André Simon remarked *that they were sold with the vendor's word of honour as their sole guarantee*, and in *The Gentleman's Cellar*, L.H. Feuerheerd even went so far as to say that he *doubted any totally pure Champagne wine from a single year was ever bottled.*

From 1830, the vintage was occasionally marked on the label for Anglo-Saxon markets, but this did not become a regular practice until the 1860's, and even a little later for Mumm. At the same time, the vintage of an exceptional year was indicated on bottles destined for other markets, France included, such as "Sparkling Sillery of 1842, P.A. Mumm Best Quality." This custom was not observed earlier unfortunately, because the first sparkling wines sold by the House of Mumm were mostly from 1825, one of the great years of the century. The 1874, 1880, 1884, 1887, 1889, 1892, 1893, 1895, 1898, 1900, 1904, 1906 and 1911 vintages were declared between 1880, when the famous 1874 was released, and the beginning of Word War I. It was only in the 19th century that the sugar level of one type of champagne, although still high, was adjusted for different markets. Russian customers craved wines with 275 to 300 grams of sugar per bottle — really syrupy! Champagne "American style" had only 110 to 165 grams, "English style," 21 to 66 grams and "French style," sold in France and everywhere else except Slavic and Anglo-Saxon countries, 165 to 200 grams per bottle, that is, fifteen to twenty times more than *brut* champagne today.

The French were content because they drank champagne with dessert,

▷ Montagne de Reims
vineyards
on the eve of the harvest.

but the English, from the beginning of the 19th century, served champagne throughout the entire meal, thus creating a demand for drier wines. In his 1835 publication, *The Original,* Thomas Walker advised that *champagne should be offered right at the beginning of dinner, and placed on the table so everyone may serve themselves as they please.* It was some years before G.H. Mumm and Co. produced a drier champagne especially for the British and North Americans, sold as *Dry* from 1880 and *Extra Dry* from the following year. An even drier *Vin Brut Extra* was released on these markets in 1881. In 1896 Mumm registered a neck label bearing the words *The Brut,* and in 1897, a label, *The Brut — G.H. Mumm and Co. Brut,* meant wine which had been disgorged and left in its natural state. *After fermentation in bottle had taken place, there was almost no sugar left in the wine - it was undrinkable, except when it came from years of exceptional quality and vinosity, or even when it was drunk very old.* Even champagne labelled *brut* for Anglo-Saxon markets, according to Vizetelly, contained up to 30 grams of sugar per bottle.

Dry champagne only began to offer any real competition to the traditional, strongly-sweetend variety in France from 1910. In 1855, when Guy de Maupassant's *Bel-Ami* dined at the Café Riche with Madame de Mareuil, he still begged for *ice cold champagne, the best — I mean sweet champagne !* From 1888, Mumm sold a champagne *sec* on the French market, and two years later, a *très sec* . At the same time the company launched a *demi-sec* champagne, a little drier than its traditional wines, but still very sweet, labelled as "rich" for Anglo-Saxon countries.

Prior to 1914, Champagne Mumm's labels kept up with changing fashion. From 1840, perhaps even earlier, they bore an eagle, which appeared again on the cork: this being the emblem of Napoléon III, it represented the summit of refined taste during his reign. Mumm's coat of arms, on which the eagle rested, was discontinued fairly quickly. Mumm produced very few labels commemorating historic occasions, like the centennial of the Revolution for example, preferring to always have the brand prominently displayed, even though certain Houses, up till the middle of the 19th century, did not.

The name, of course, fluctuated with changes in the firm: "P. A. Mumm and Co." was followed by in 1853 by "G. H. Mumm and Co.," with "G. de Bary," one of the owners between 1853 and 1875, added from 1903. For a long time the word "champagne" was not mentioned on the label: like other producers, Mumm used to call its wines "Ay Sparkling," "Sillery Sparkling," "Verzenay Sparkling" etc. Ay or Aï had been famous for its wines since the 16th century. In a letter addressed to the Count of Olonne, Saint-Evremond wrote: *Wine from Ay is the most natural and healthiest wine there is; it has little trace of earthiness and a most exquisitely delightful peach taste, which is characteristic of it and, in my opinion, the best of all flavours. Léon XIII, Charles Quint, Francois Ier, Henry VIII all had their own houses in Ay or nearby to have more convenient access to their wine supplies. With all the important world affairs that these princes had to deal with, supplying themselves with wine from Ay was still a significant consideration.*

Sillery owes its fame to a great nobleman, Nicolas Brulart de Sillery, chancellor to Henri IV, and his descendants. Of these, Adélaïde, wife of the Marshall of Estrées, is remembered for having tended her vines with rare intelligence and devotion; on her death her vineyard was named *Clos de la Maréchale.*

On reflection, it was a very strange custom to put a vineyard name on a bottle of champagne, since very little or none of its character would have been present after blending. This tradition survived however until 1914, though from the time of Napoléon III, the main producers still added *grand*

53

mousseux, mousseux or *crémant* to the word "champagne," a practice which did not completely die out until the beginning of the 20th century. Trying several approaches at once, Mumm launched a Cabinet champagne 1884 Verzenay, after registering a label carrying the word "champagne" for Anglo-Saxon markets in 1881.

The word "cabinet" was used in both French and English, referring to individual private salons, very much in fashion at the time: *Between three and four o'clock in the morning, waiters with ice buckets and bottles of champagne ran around non-stop; they looked like they were putting out a fire* was Charles Monselet's description in his *Lettres Gourmandes* of 1877. Labels carried inscriptions which were supposed to indicate quality, but most were purely whimsical. Taking Mumm's labels for example, if *Grand Vin* was a great wine, and *Qualité Supérieure* a top *cuvée*, what were "Exquisite Quality," "Unequalled," "The Flower of Sillery," "The Cream of Bouzy," or "Royal Rosé" supposed to mean?

The vintage and *dosage* were displayed on the main, back or neck label and, from 1890, *demi-sec* was named Carte Blanche. Cordon Rouge, rapidly to become synonymous with the name Mumm, had appeared some years before.

The father of Welby Jourdan, Mumm's Paris agent, had an ingenious idea in the 1870's and advised Georges Hermann von Mumm: *Go ahead and decorate your bottles with the Légion d'honneur, sales will rocket!* From 1876, as a trial and in order to honour certain important French and foreign clients, several bottles had a red silk ribbon wrapped around their neck, whose ends crossed and were sealed with an oval label bearing the words

Cordon Rouge. On 16 November, 1876, name and label were registered at the Rheims business court.

Mumm's United States agent did likewise, adding a back label, "Selected Brut." The ribbon, of no practical use, was abandoned in favour of a label, registered in Rheims on 22 March, 1883, with the words *Cordon Rouge* inscribed in large golden letters on a wide diagonal red band in modern-style lettering. The vintage was indicated on the label — 1889, 1893 etc. — if there was room. Curiously, this had been registered two years earlier in New York, probably on the initiative of the American importer.

On 7 June, 1907, Mumm renewed registration of the brand *Cordon Rouge* in advance, and this time, a green sash was provided to differentiate *demi-sec* champagne. In 1924 a double sash even appeared — red and green — for *sec.*

Cordon Rouge was an established success from the beginning of the century. Its coloured sash was delightfully reminiscent of the ancient Royal and Military Order of Saint Louis, known before the Revolution as the *Cordon Rouge.* But the most striking similarity was with the *Grand Cordon* of the Légion d'honneur, worn by French presidents: between the wars there was even a G.H. Mumm and Co. poster depicting Napoléon I decorating a bottle of Mumm with the sash in question.

In France, Cordon Rouge featured on the 1901 price list of Dubonnet and Co.; overseas, it very rapidly gained an enviable reputation. In *L'Assiette au Beurre* of 15 February, 1902, was a Jacques Villon sketch of a reveller holding aloft a bottle of Cordon Rouge. This became a rallying sign for wine-lovers, who began ordering: "A bottle of Cordon Rouge!" Ever since then, it has signified for many, simply "champagne." In more recent times, there has been further testimony of this in comic strips. In *Objectif Lune*, a Tintin

adventure, a bottle of Cordon Rouge was used, and Uderzo, in *Astérix*, naturally painted a red stripe across Roman amphoras, to show they contained champagne.

In just under a century, Mumm had set up the structure and means of efficient production; the prestigious reputation of the brand was beyond any doubt due in large measure to the excellent quality of its wines. But simply making good wines was not enough, they had to be sold - Mumm had to find its own niche in the market in the face of well-entrenched competitors. The champagne business was on the one hand assisted by the growing fortunes of the bourgeoisie and Napoléon III's free-trade initiatives, but on the other, confronted with no end of troublesome problems.

During the 19th century, a series of wars, changes of governments and economic policies on both sides of the Atlantic destabilised champagne sales. The economic slumps of 1846, 1858 and 1873 left very deep scars. Champagne weathered the first of these well, in contrast to other French wine regions, whose sales fell sharply. But in 1858, the American market was severely affected, and in 1873, the repercussions of some very serious German bankruptcies were felt throughout Europe and the United States. There was concern over the sizeable drop in Champagne exports and, although they were back to normal in 1885, they suffered another setback in 1892 due to a general rise in customs duties when France abandoned its free trade policy.

Champagne was always subject to numerous duties and taxes, whatever the circumstances: the *Vigneron Champenois* of 24 March, 1888, lists thirteen. A *Petition of vineyard owners in the Epernay and Châlons districts* of 1829 *noted the discreet presence of the authorities, there to harass merchants, and who kept anyone connected with wine in any way constantly on their*

guard. It deplored *the necessity for a carrier to stop in every village he went through and pay for a transit pass* specifying that *a single wicker basket of 12 bottles, dispatched from Epernay to the most distant border, would stop at the entrance and exit of 29 towns.* Being considered a luxury product, champagne regularly attracted heavy customs duties, more noticeably in certain periods, when it was a way for other countries to retaliate against France's protectionnist policy or, if it produced its own sparkling wine, to protect it against competition from champagne. At the end of the 19th century, a bottle of Mumm which sold for 5 francs in Paris, was liable for 3.50 francs customs duty in the United States, and 4.76 francs in Russia.

One of the everpresent problems of the champagne business was the irregularity of the grape harvest. Supply depended on a production which was too often insufficient, or non-existent, as was the case in 1854, 1859, 1879, 1908 and 1910. Producers had to pay very high prices and compete for a share of the poor harvest. Wine supply could not keep up with demand: in this respect, what was true in the 19th century also holds true today.

The then precarious state of transport was another hurdle to overcome. Land communications were slow and sometimes difficult due to bad road maintenance; mail delivery and shipments both suffered. In its first years of existence, Mumm used transport agents, such as Marcelin, the carrier from Châlons, who delivered its champagne to Marseille; shorter distances, notably Rheims - Epernay, were covered by a transport firm in Montchenot, and small quantities were sent by stage-coach. Three itineraries were established for Switzerland, passing through Bâle, Pontarlier or Lyon. In 1840, carrier charges were 0.4 franc per bottle, in other words, nearly 8 % of the production price. Consignment notes had to be sent to Châlons-sur-Marne to be stamped, giving rise to additional delays. No end of complications! Labels for Russia had to be sent separately to Marseille by stage-coach, in a parcel bearing a lead seal from the Russian consulate!

In the 1850's, the arrival of railways simplified trading, and champagne could at last be sent to Paris via the Rheims-Epernay line. All the same, trains then did not travel at the same speed as they do today. According to the *Vigneron Champenois* of 1 March, 1899, parcels took 17 days to travel from Paris to Marseille! Horses still carried champagne on big flat waggons from Mumm's cellars to the Rheims railway station.

Under Louis-Phillipe, canals from the Marne to the Aisne and the Marne to the Rhine were opened up. Water was, in fact, a very traditional method of transporting champagne; from the 18th century, hampers destined for Paris and Rouen had been shipped from Mareuil-sur-Ay, and Mumm used this method from 1827. Canals were also important for supplying firms with empty bottles.

Sea routes too were dangerous. Shipwrecks were common and in its first trading year, P. A. Mumm lost a large cargo, loaded in Rouen on "La Seine," which went down in the seas off Jutland. Rouen was the port of lading for Hamburg, Rostock, Elseneur and Saint-Petersburg. Shipments for London went via Calais; for Dublin, Belfast and Bristol via Le Havre and La Rochelle; for Odessa, via Marseille. Although Belgium was usually supplied by land, it also received shipments from Dunkerque.

The arrival of steam transformed both land and sea communications. In 1830 it took, on average, 40 days to go from Le Havre to New York, but by 1870, the same passage took no more than a week. Steamers participated indirectly in champagne promotion: considerable quantities were drunk on board, and maritime companies such as Austrian Lloyd and The American Maritime Company had their own *cuvée* of Mumm. One of Mumm's most beautiful labels depicts a huge steamer with 6 masts and a chimney; the inscription reads: *Ordered expressly for the steamers of the Great-Western Steam-Ship Company*. It also extended warm wishes for: *a happy, pleasant and quick passage*.

During wartime, transport was very obviously disrupted, when it existed at all. On 10 August, 1827, M. Heuser wrote to his shipper in Marseille, R. Nicolas, to ask him to estimate the dangers to shipments to Odessa via Constantinople, and made inquiries about *current insurance prices*. At a later date, Heuser was worried about the likelihood that ships would be laid up over winter in Constantinople by temperatures which would damage the champagne. Letters were exchanged, there were hesitations, and then it was decided to load the freight amidships for maximum protection. Imagine the delays involved in this exchange of correspondence, by stage-coach from Rheims to Marseille and then by sailing ship, and back again under the same conditions! During the 1870 Franco-Prussian war, railways were commandeered and canal flood-gates destroyed, so internal transport was carried out by horse-drawn vehicles. Exports were transported by road, then Belgian rail to Anvers; champagne shipments ended up congesting the port so much that deliveries had to be slowed down.

Due to slow transport, champagne could be exposed to cold or inclement weather, with the risk of tartrate crystals precipitating or even bottles breaking; hot weather was equally damaging. On 23 July, 1827, M. Heuser wrote to a customer in Vervey: *The Spring and autumn are more suitable for shipping Champagne wines, which are damaged to the same degree by weather which is too hot or too cold.*

Wines were packed therefore, in wicker baskets at that time, with particular care. Mumm had a range of sizes, holding 30, 40, 50 and 60 bottles,

whose prices varied between 4.50 francs and 7 francs. Wooden cases holding 25, 30, 36, 40, 50, 60, 72, 80 and 100 bottles, and costing from 9 to 18 francs were used for deliveries to more distant destinations. Both wicker-baskets and cases were fitted internally with sheets of cardboard and straw packing, each bottle being wrapped in paper and protected by a sheath of straw or, from 1866, a mechanically manufactured straw-case. This type of packing continued to exist up till World War I, with wood, then cardboard, gradually replacing wicker.

Champagne producers had to struggle against growing competition from foreign wines, this song of Abel Sallé describing the menacing invasion:

Gourmets, where do you get your manic desire
To travel far and wide searching for wines
Outside your own country?
Greece, Africa and Spain
Have access to your feasts and banquets
Driving out champagne
Heavens above, you are not French!

The most serious was certainly the confusim in the consumer's mind between champagne and sparkling wine, which brazenly stole its name. In his *Essay on the History of the Wines of Champagne* of 1845, Max Sutaine wrote: *Champagne wine has suffered the same fate as all great successful discoveries; a crowd of imitations has rushed headlong in its wake, and fraudulent imitations have jumped on and clung to the fashion bandwagon it has created. The press spoke of wine of Champagne produced by the Côte*

△ *Bottling.*

d'Or, and in the *Moniteur Viticole* of 28 December, 1873, it reported: *In Saumur, champagne sales are fairly brisk!*

Sparkling wine had existed in France from 1820, and also in Germany, who learned the method from the Swiss, who had been making sparkling wine since the 18th century. Russia made "Krimska champagne" in Crimea and "Donski champagne" in the valley of the Don. The United States produced sparkling wine from 1837; Italy, Spain and Austria from the middle of the century. To copy champagne and borrow its name was one thing, but some borrowed the names of the great champagne Houses. This fraud became widespread, and went so far as to label the latest batch of sparkling wine with a famous champagne brand of the customer's choice! This resulted in a *Petition of wine merchants and wine producers of Champagne*, which had no definitive result. In 1857, a law was enacted to defend commercial and manufacturing brand-names, but its provisions were too lax, and did not prevent trade-marks being registered by manufacturers outside Champagne. Mumm joined forces with other producers to bring legal action against imposters. From 1882, they were supported by the Association of Champagne Wine Merchants and, with its patronage, five Houses, including G.H. Mumm and Co., obtained damages from sparkling wine producers in Vienna and Budapest who had pirated their brands. Other actions were also successful, in France at least. Mumm owed its success, as well, to a good commercial organisation of salespeople, brokers and agents of great dynamism and untiring energy.

The firm's owners and members of the management team, by their personal actions, extended the reputation of the brand. They made uncomfortable voyages, even to snowbound areas of Russia and Canada, when bogged carriages on roads in an appalling state of repair, highway robbers,

△ *Disgorging.*

rats and bed bugs at inns along the way, and shipwrecks at sea were common occurrences. Partners were directly involved in business negotiations, such as M. Giesler, who moved to London from 1827 to acquire a better knowledge of the English market. Some were members of the Mumm companies in Frankfurt and Cologne which, by providing champagne for their clientele, contributed for many years to the French firm's success.

Salesmen and brokers, but particularly agents, were very proud of their brand, since it was rapidly recognised as one of the finest in Champagne. The Chilean agent, for example, put up a poster on the kiosk of the main square in Cochabamba, saying: *Mumm, la primera marca de champagne del Mundo!* At the beginning of this century, twenty or so agents represented the company — four in Germany and three in Russia. Elsewhere, they were less specialised, some responsible for a group of countries, for example, Austria and Hungary being the responsibility of the Vienna agent, Argentina, Uruguay and Paraguay, of the agent in Buenos Aires. Agents' budgets varied considerably according to their importance. In 1907, the London agent received 108,700 francs for the year, the Riga agent.....856 francs. In numerous countries "exclusive importers" were appointed, their names appearing on a back label. They covered all or part of a country, or were responsible for several countries.

Champagne salesmen in France were considered to be the best in the business. This charming description was given in 1841, in *How the French See Themselves* by Aldolphe Ricard: *Commercial travellers for quality Champagne wine have nothing in common with Burgundy brokers of Bercy and their cavalier behaviour. They dine at Véfour, have a horror of drunkeness and speak of their wares in moderate tones only. They generally conduct business in private salons, on public promenades or in the foyer of the Opéra.*

After extolling the virtues of sparkling champagne in an elegant manner, they always end the encounter by saying with an innocent air: "I will send you a case, but, for goodness sake, don't consider yourself under any obligation to keep it." With that, they button up their white gloves, or play with their lorgnon. The subject of Aï wine is then dropped, and the topic of conversation changed to Lord Seymour's horses, or the mineral water of Bagnères.

Mumm had a first-class, loyal clientele, among them great wine merchants, the best hotels and restaurants, including "night clubs" when they appeared, as well as clubs and circles. Many had their own reserved *cuvée*, with a back label saying: "Consigned for," "Reserve of," "Specially Shipped for," or simply mentioning the establishment.

In addition to being traditional champagne supplier to the aristocracy and upper middle class, Mumm, as we have seen, also supplied royalty. The Austro-Hungarian, Belgian, Dutch, Prussian, Danish, Swedish, Norwegian, and English courts, not to mention the Grand Dukes of Oldenbourg and Hesse-Darmstadt, all featured in the accounts of the 1890's. This prestigious honour was proudly exhibited on a special label "Champagne of Sovereigns G.H. Mumm and Co. — Rheims," displaying their illustrious clients' coats of arms.

Considerable amounts of money were spent by the House of Mumm on brand promotion, as demonstrated by the 1907 accounts. This included advertising, press releases, gifts of champagne to the diplomatic corps (100 bottles for its annual dinner) and to various associations (100 bottles for a banquet of the German community, with which Mumm had a particular affinity), gifts in cash or champagne to the restaurant trade and wine waiters (*maîtres d'hôtels* and wine waiters of the Jockey Club and the Wine Waiters' Association). In addition there was the cost of printed menus and "advertising giveaways," pearl

handled knives, pens and propelling pencils, inkwells, cigar-cutters, wallets and notebooks covered in celluloid. Overseas agents extended the company's promotional efforts: the same accounts recorded that the Prussian agent donated a gift in aid of the Deprived Children's Fund, and the Chilean agent graciously furnished bottles for the Santiago horse races. Some were clearly excellent public relations people.

Mumm participated in national, regional and international exhibitions, particularly the latter, very much in vogue in the 19th century, either under its own name or as a member of the Association of Champagne Merchants. The latter was the case at the Paris World Fairs of 1889 and 1900, where the Association was housed in a prestigious Rococo style "Champagne Palace" designed by the Rheims architect, Kalas. There were public displays of *remuage* and *dégorgement* and, at the stands, 1 franc would buy a glass of champagne carrying the Association's label and a neck label with the words "1900 World Fair." Producers' names did not feature on labels, but a daily tasting of champagnes of participating Houses took place on a rotating basis. At both the 1889 and 1900 exhibitions, the collective Champagne presentation received the highest award of the event.

Having resolutely chosen to make quality their keynote, Mumm's prices were relatively high from the beginning: in 1827, rosé champagne was being sold on the French market at 2.75 francs wholesale, whereas Mumm was charging 3.50 francs.

In the Belle Epoque, there were three varieties of Mumm champagne, with varying *dosage levels* — Carte Blanche (sweet), "Extra-Dry" (dry) and Cordon Rouge (very dry). Their 1901 retail prices were 7.50 francs to 8 francs, 8.40 francs to 9 francs and 9.40 francs to 9.50 francs respectively.

On the eve of World War I, Mumm's sales overall were 3 million bottles,

△ *"Master,*
one does not drink
Mumm Champagne, one savors it."

9 % of total champagne sales: it was number one in the business. Every market was different, however. In 1913, Mumm sold almost 200,000 bottles in France, less than the total amount sold abroad, but more than in any individual market with the exception of the United States and Russia. In any case, consumption in France served as a springboard for worldwide expansion because a lot of foreigners were in France in the 19th century, and even more at the beginning of the 20th. The story goes that, at Maxim's, *the Grand-Duke Ivan drank eight bottles of Mumm one after the other before passing out cold (*Gault et Millau, *"La Belle Epoque")*. It was in this famous establishment, at the very beginning of the century, that René Lalou, a regular customer and future president of Mumm, refused to pay a supplement of 1 franc to have his champagne served chilled. In those prosperous years, the French were among the most enthusiastic champagne drinkers, and Mumm's agents spent an enormous amount of energy in positioning the brand at the top and keeping it there, notably the Paris agent, M. Jourdan, the famous "Welby," M. Trémoulière's partner from 1902. The former flattered himself on having drunk 40,000 bottles of champagne — Mumm of course — over the course of his 94 years, a diet which obviously suited him! M. Trémoulière did not lag very far behind him, if his diaries are to be believed. On 3 February, 1900, he lunched at Prunier's where he drank a bottle of Cordon Rouge 1893, by himself apparently. At the Larue bar, he then drank two bottles of Mumm 1895 with Welby Jourdan and a customer as an aperitif. Invited to dinner at Durand's by M. Denis Mounié, he brought along four bottles three quarters full, then later took two of the guests to the Casino de Paris, where a further three bottles were drunk at the Polasky bar. The evening finally wound up at Tabarin's, where another three bottles were demolished. What devotion to duty! What stamina!

In the 19th century champagne was an integral part of the good life, whether associated with the escapades of romantic bohemians, the festivities of the Second Empire, or the sophisticated parties of the end-of-the-century's golden youth. While attending the Special Military School of Saint-Cyr in 1876, the future Sahara explorer, hermit and priest — the extravagant Viscount Charles de Foucauld — would drink a chilled bottle of Mumm, specially reserved for wine lovers, at the Café Anglais every Sunday. But what description could do justice to the way champagne flowed in the Belle Epoque? It was its Golden Age, and Cordon Rouge the rallying cry among the champagne devotees of gay Parisian life. Its corks popped everywhere: it was drunk by both revellers and bourgeoisie, and featured on the Jules Chéret poster created for the Taverne Olympia as well as the cover of the edition of *L'Assiette au Beurre* of 29 April, 1911, dedicated to the Champagne growers' revolt.

The menu for guests of the *Complimentary Dinner given 17 February, 1902 at the Restaurant Julien, under the gracious presidency of Mlle Polaire of "Bouffes-Parisiens" and M. Albert Carré, director of the Opéra-Comique* designed by the great artist Jacques Villon, depicted two pretty women in raptures as a bottle decorated with the famous sash was presented. Jules Roques, founder and director of the *Courrier Français,* wished each of his friends, for the year 1907, *365 nights of happiness and to hell with the rest,* in a magnificent greeting card drawn by Willette of an attractively draped naked horsewoman, togetherwith a bottle of Cordon Rouge. Cordon Rouge also featured on postcards when they became available. There is one with a bottle on the pedestal table of a boudoir, and a rakish young man offering a glass to a young woman in a suggestive manner — the caption explains all:

There is more chance of a kiss
When intoxicated by joyous champagne!

Before 1914, true champagne lovers existed only in the privileged classes, and producers strove to cater to their tastes and gain their loyalty. They gave wholehearted support to aviation weeks arranged in Champagne in 1909 and 1910 as public relations exercises, an initiative well ahead of their time. Aviation, at that time, was fuelled by the willingness and enthusiasm of exceptional men. The association between champagne, wine of success, and the conquest of the air was a natural one: champagne was what was drunk to celebrate victorious flight landings. From 1905, even before Farman had flown his one kilometre stretch (Bouzy-Rheims), the association between champagne and aviation had been symbolised by a page in *Vie Parisienne* on 28 August; it showed an enormous French rooster perched on top of a pile of airships and aeroplanes, with the astonishing caption: *It is you, Clicquot, Mumm, Roederer, Moët and Pommery who have conquered the air! Every French rooster in the country is crowing that Champagne wine is the best fuel.*

Four years later, champagne and aviation sealed their alliance on the ground. The "Great Week of Champagne" was held on the plain of Bétheny, near Rheims, from 22 to 29 August, 1909. Due to the generosity of the champagne trade and people of Rheims, 220,000 francs of prize money was offered. Mumm donated a "Pilot's Prize," awarded to the fastest airship over five circuits of the course. This was organised by the Marquis de Polignac, head of Pommery, assisted by leading Champagne merchants, including Hermann de Mumm: Raoul de Bary was vice-president of the organisation committee.

The idea itself was an audacious one, because handling aeroplanes was still a very risky business. At Rheims and Epernay, flagpoles flew black, white or red pennants signifying "no start," "possible start" or "definite start," depending on the weather. Thirty-eight machines took part, and it was a resounding success. Blériot, who had just crossed the Channel, beat the ten kilometre record, averaging 70 km/hour, and the American, Curtis, at almost 75 km/hour, broke the speed record. The distance record was beaten successively by Paulhan (113 km), Latham (154 km) and Farman (190 km). On the last day, Latham attempted to break the altitude record. According to *L'Almanach Matot-Braine* of 1910, *the plane soared to a stupendous height, kept on climbing and rose up again to the point where it appeared no larger than a fly; in the stands, a frenetic cheer welcomed this impressive flight which finished off the week with such audacity and sang-froid.* The pilot reached a height of 155 meters.

Armand Fallières, the French President, and Prince Albert of Belgium were guests of honour. Champagne flowed, *L'Illustration* of the 4 September reporting that *a great deal of it was drunk at the buffet in the stands, one of the triumphs of Bétheny.* From 3 to 10 July, 1910, the "Great Aviation Week of Champagne" took place according to the same formula, but on an even larger scale. Walther de Mumm participated in the aviation trials in two "Antoinette" monoplanes. The success of 1909 was repeated, although the death of the pilot, Wachter, and the injuries sustained by Mme de Laroche, the only woman in the event, cast a gloom over proceedings. Records were re-established at 106 km/h for speed, 340 km for distance and 1,150 metres for altitude by the 76 machines which took part. What progress in one year! The word champagne was on everyone's lips, as it had been in 1909.

Great Britain was consistently the main champagne importer, and was thus given top priority by Champagne merchants: the English seemed to

have concluded a permanent alliance with champagne. During the 18th century and up till 1815, despite wars and the disorder they created, no obstacle was allowed to interfere with the flow of exports across the Channel, even if it meant shipping by round-about routes, via the Channel Islands or Holland. From the 1820's, permanent peace allowed normal routing of champagne and, from March 1827, P.A. Mumm and Co. shipped to London, Liverpool, Bristol and Ireland. In 1829, its "Fine Sparkling Champagne 1825" enjoyed great success in London, helped by the fine reputation of the firm's Moselle and Rhine wines there.

Since its foundation, Mumm had taken a special interest in the English palate, and adapted its wine to suit it. Such experience enabled it to write the following to a hotel proprietor in Brussels on 10 October, 1827: *We know your establishment is much frequented by the English and are taking the liberty of drawing to your attention that we know exactly the type of wine these gentlemen prefer. We can say without presumption, that our wine already enjoys a great reputation in England.* Mumm rapidly rose to become one of the leading brands on the English market. In 1855, an 1842 bottle of Mumm was sold at auction at Christie's for 62 shillings, an extremely high price for the time. A book entitled *Champagne* relates that, in 1880, *Mumm's name had been familiar for over half a century to wine merchants and wine lovers* and that its champagnes *were excellent wines which could hold their own in comparison with any of their top competitors.*

This reputation was owed in part to producing dry champagne which the English preferred. In 1879, it launched an "Extra Dry," *a perfectly "dry" version of "Carte Blanche," which was pale, delicate, and creamy, with a delightful bouquet and refined flavour.* In 1880, it followed this with an "Extra Brut Wine G.H. Mumm and Co. — Special Reserve for Great

△ *Hermann de Mumm*
member of the Commitee
for the "Grande Semaine d'Aviation"
(Rheims, August 1909)
and Walther de Mumm,
aviator.

Britain" and in 1900, Cordon Rouge was introduced, advertised as *the most expensive, therefore the best.*

As one of the favourites of the Royal household, champagne Mumm was present at all Buckingham Palace receptions; it was, for example, served at the Derby Day Banquet of 1904. That same year, 250,000 bottles of top quality champagne were shipped across the Channel, *the best champagnes of the finest producers always being reserved for the English market.*

Champagne was not very well-known in North America in the 18th century, nor even at the beginning of the 19th, despite Samuel Johnson reporting that *an excellent champagne* was served on 4 March, 1790, at a dinner given at the White House. The American champagne market emerged in the 1820's, and demand in this young nation escalated very rapidly. Combined exports to the United States and Canada had reached 400,000 bottles by 1832, making North America the third largest champagne importer. On 3 March 1829, two years after it was founded, Mumm shipped 1,764 bottles of "sparkling white wine" to New York on the "Charlemagne." Transatlantic sales grew very quickly, and Patrick Forbes notes that from the 1850's, there were few periods during which the firm was not number one exporter to the United States. Vizetelly elaborated on this in 1879: *Messieurs G.H. Mumm and Co. hold the leading position for exports to the United States, where their products are held in high regard, with nearly half a million bottles, a quarter of the total shipments to that country.* The author of *Champagne* verified that *no House of the "champagne trade" even approached Mumm for volume of annual exports to the United States.* In 1882, Bertall calculated in *La Vigne* that if champagne Houses *shared out, so to speak, the main world areas of interest, Mumm's territory would be the whole of America* — Canada included apparently. According to statistics,

▷ *Mumm labels
from different periods
throughout the world.*

"MUMM's Extra dry"
The Champion.

Mumm sent 420,000 bottles to the United States in 1877 and 1,500,000 bottles in 1902, its best year for that market. North America, at that time, was the second largest champagne market after England, and Mumm's success in the New Continent was so great that the company constructed special cellars at 34 and 36 rue du Champ-de-Mars reserved for packing American shipments.

Mumm champagne was found all over the United States, including the red-light district of New Orleans, and the "small private salons," where Extra Dry *gushed forth. In the main cities it seemed as firmly established an institution as it was in Paris, and* it was claimed that *the New England custom for lovers to eat a piece of maple sugar until their lips met had been replaced by lovers drinking champagne from the same glass.* Even gold prospectors transformed the nuggets they discovered in the sand or mud of mountain streams into bottles of Cordon Rouge.

And yet, selling in North America was no easy accomplishment! The odds were very much against establishing a market on a continent so vast, with such a diversity of populations. Although most people were interested in enjoying life, puritan leagues vigorously opposed the consumption of alcohol, maintaining that "intoxicating beverages" led to the degeneration of races and misery for families. Their members, who were persuaded it was up to them to fight against that, had the support of feminist leagues, the clergy and part of the medical fraternity. In 1853, believe it or not, the American Society for the Promotion of Temperance had the traditional bottle of champagne replaced by a bottle of water at the launching of "The Great Republic."

As in every other country, economic downturns and difficult times affected champagne sales. Scarcely had they recovered from the slump of

▷ *Cordon Rouge
Symphony.*

1858, than the War of Secession slowed them down once more. The world-wide depression of 1873 struck a savage blow and, in 1890, the Hispano-American War caused sales to drop by 50 %.

Customs duties, high everywhere, were particularly steep here. They could be as much as 70 % of the ex-cellars price, to which sea freight charges and large profit margins had to be added. As far as champagne imitations were concerned, the United States beat all records for creative inventiveness. It refused to abide by the Paris Joint Trade Agreement, and American sparkling wines continued to be erroneously called "champagne." In 1908: *Illinois "champagnes" are found on all the best tables of the United States. A new district founded there, situated in a white wine-producing area (fortunately), making sparkling wines with cheeky French-style labels, has been named Rheims. A gallant female French cook whose name happens to be, by a stroke of providence, Madame Veuve Pommery, has agreed to come to this American town of Rheims.*

North America offered the advantages of a non-saturated market in a continent where wealth grew rapidly and people took delight in displaying it. The owners of Mumm visited the country itself to decide what strategy to follow and, even when the United States had been successfully won over, its directors continued to visit, Hermann de Mumm, for example, in 1903. Georges Robinet, responsible for Anglo-Saxon markets, crossed the Atlantic many times in the same period. Being aware of the American taste for spectacular gestures, he used to invite fifteen or so well-chosen passengers during the voyage to a formal dinner in a small private salon. As soon as introductions were completed, a case of Extra-Dry or Cordon Rouge was

MENU

La Soupe du " Courrier français "
Les Carpes à la Chambord
Agneau rôti
Haricots blancs gratinés
Foies gras en terrine
Salade de saison
Poires des Présidentes
Entremets Pihan
Fromages — Fruits

VINS

Chablis 1re
Médoc vieux
Clos-Ponchon
G.-H. Mumm Cordon Rouge
Curaçao Bols blanc

—

Distribution de Surprises

27me. "DINER DE FAVEUR"

donné le Vendredi 23 Janvier 1903

SOUS LA PRÉSIDENCE DE

M. JULES ROQUES

Directeur du " Courrier français "

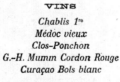

Dessins de Louis Morin et Widhopff.

opened. His American companions exclaimed with delight, and remained in raptures throughout the entire dinner, after which they retired to their cabins.......ecstatic and conquered.

The choice of United States agent was a delicate issue for Mumm, which entered the American market at a time when some of its competitors were already enviably well-entrenched. The first was John G. & E. Boker & Co. of New York. Frédérick de Bary, a brother of Guillaume and Albert, directors of G.H. Mumm and Co., then moved to New York and set up the firm of "F. de Bary & Co.," which became Mumm's United States agent in 1852. Its role was a determining factor in the brand's success in 1911, it is replaced by "Mumm Champagne & Importation Company" and represented there by a certain Mr Renken. It was the job of the company's agents to tactfully approach people of rank and distinction who might be interested in the product and help in its promotion, whether they be Senators, or sporting personalities, such as Wilbur Wright Aero-Club members who were given 100 bottles of champagne in 1907. Walter R. Wonham & Sons of Montréal was an excellent agent for Canada in this respect.

Another consideration was the American palate. Until the 1850's, Mumm was shipping the same champagnes to the United States, that is "Pierry Mousseux," "Ay Mousseux," "Verzenay Mousseux," "Sillery Grand Mousseux" and "Œil-de-Perdrix Mousseux," but wine lovers across the Atlantic soon begged for champagne labelled "dry" to drink with meals, then later "extra-dry" and even "brut." Paradoxically, these champagnes were sweeter than identically-labelled champagnes on the English market; in 1880, "American style" still had an average sugar content of 140 grams per litre! Some bottles had labels specifying "For America only" or "American style," others labelled their champagne with American names, such as

82

◁ The delight of illustrators
◁◁ and connoisseurs.

"Cherokee Rose G.H. Mumm and Co. Reims-Expressly Prepared for Redwood & Sons, Mobile."

Cordon Rouge was so well-known by the time it appeared on the American market, that a composer named Edmund Walsieffer wrote a piece entitled *Cordon Rouge Gallop*, published in Philadelphia in three versions — for piano, for orchestra and for brass band. In 1905, when a drier version of Cordon Rouge was officially launched in New York, dry champagne was at the height of fashion and Mumm thus became, in the United States as well as Canada, the symbol of champagne itself. Vizetelly described its significance in Anglo-Saxon countries as follows: *its success in oiling the wheels of social life is so profound and so universally recognised that its disappearance would almost signify a breakdown of the social system.*

In its early days in Germany and Austria/Hungary, Mumm took advantage of its well-established connections with Frankfurt and Cologne, where champagne had been appreciated from the beginning of the 18th century. Goethe made abundant reference to this fact in *Wilhelm Meister*. Later Hoffman, in *The Magnetiser*, wrote that *all dreams are made of froth* but that *this can only be true if we mean the most noble froth of all, that of exuberant, fizzy, gassy, bubbling, sparkling, impetuous champagne.* For a long time the German and the Rheims firms had common agents, which led at times to confusion. *L'Illustration* of 2 August, 1862, published an article entitled *Opening of the Frankfurt Rifle Range*, depicting an engraving bearing the following inscription, in large letters, on a horse-drawn wagon: *P.A. Mumm Frankfurt — Vienna Lieferung — G.H. Mumm and Co. Rheims — Champagne — Depôt, Boulevard des Italiens, 50 — Paris.* In 1871 an agreement stipulated that a certain Mr Goeden was *in charge of selling in the French provinces, then occupied by German troops, and annexed Alsace-Lorraine,*

▷ *New labels of Cordon Rouge after 1918.*

Dessin de E. VIRTEL

LA PLUS HAUTE QUALITÉ
caractérise
les CHAMPAGNES G.H. MUMM & Cº

SOCIÉTÉ VINICOLE DE CHAMPAGNE Propriétaire

REIMS

not only the champagne of G.H. Mumm and Co., but also the wines of P.A. Mumm, Frankfurt. He was required to *devote all his zeal and energy to the sale of wines of the aforementioned Houses and not to sell other sparkling wines or wines from the Rhine and Moselle, except those coming from the aforementioned Houses of Rheims and Frankfurt.* The Rheims company however, gradually became independent, and organised its own distribution network on the other side of the Rhine. By 1908 it had agents in Hamburg, Berlin, Vienna, and even Frankfurt and Cologne, and by 1913 was exporting 150,000 bottles to Germany, and 70,000 to Austria/Hungary.

In the 19th century, Russia flung its doors open to champagne, after Russian troops occupying France in 1815 had brought it back in their

△ *The Grand Tir*
de Francfort
(L'Illustration, 1862).

wagons. The same applied in Belgium which, by the end of the century, drank more champagne per head than any other nation. The same year it was founded, P.A. Mumm and Co. shipped bottles to Saint Petersburg, Odessa, Riga and Dantzig, supplying Liège and Anvers, as well as Holland, via Givet and La Meuse. Scandinavia, Italy and Switzerland were also among the company's best markets. Later on, a special effort was made to woo Russia. Charles Monselet stated at this time, in *La Cuisinière Poétique*, that *at that great Moscow restaurant, the Novo Troitskoï Traktir, meals are always accompanied by chilled champagne, the inevitable basis of every Russian meal eaten in the finest of company*. Mumm therefore selected someone to handle its affairs in Russia — the son of one of its directors, Max von Guaïta, whose mother came from an important Moscow wine merchant family. In 1913, through its agents in Odessa, Saint Petersburg, Moscow, Riga and Warsaw, Mumm sold 350,000 bottles to Russia and 82,000 in annexed Poland.

By the beginning of the 20th century, G.H. Mumm and Co. was exporting 100,000 bottles annually to South America (60 % to Argentina), 60,000 to Belgium, 44,000 to Sweden and the same to Central America. Other significant markets were Holland, Australia, Italy and Switzerland which, in 1913, imported 28,000, 25,000, 24,000, and 17,000 bottles respectively. The accounts of the same year showed that, at the time, Champagne Mumm was established throughout the world: there were sales to Indonesia, the Philippines, Malaysia, Siam, Singapore, Ceylon, Mauritius, New Zealand — and 32,000 bottles were even shipped to... China.

▷ *Vines
in autumn.*

4

The Years of Upheaval

Even though the Mumm family lived in Champagne, Hermann von Mumm and his brothers were still German nationals. During military call-up they left for Germany, but Hermann, being too old to qualify for military service, hoped to remain in France, and so applied for French nationality. When World War I was on the point of breaking out, he gathered his staff together and gave the following speech: "I have just come back from the prefecture, war is imminent. I ask those who have been called up to do their duty as Frenchmen; I will do my duty as director. I am staying in Rheims and, while the war continues, your wives may come to the cellars at the end of each month and pick up your full salary."

But when Germany declared war on France on 3 August, 1914, Hermann von Mumm, who had still not received a reply to his request for naturalisation, was interned in Brittany at Lanvéoc fort with other Germans working in France: there they stayed in captivity till hostilities ended. His wife, the daughter of a Russian ambassador in Paris and as big a francophile as her unlucky husband, managed to get to Switzerland with the children. One of their sons remembers that, just as they crossed the border, she said: "Children, go back, we are going to sing the Marseillaise."

The company was sequestered on 28 December, 1914, and a temporary manager, M. Baudot, assigned, assisted by M. Farre, former judge at the Rheims business court. Since neither knew anything about champagne, they employed Georges Robinet, Hermann de Mumm's collaborator, as technical advisor. He stayed in Rheims during the entire war and voluntarily made sure the company was effectively run. It was no easy task to be head of a champagne House during those troubled years, with the region paying double tribute — its men away fighting, its land a battlefield. Vineyards were ploughed up with trenches, ripped apart by shells and polluted by asphyxiat-

ing gas. Men were away and horses had been requisitioned. Fertiliser, products for treatment of vines and raw materials were all scarce. Nevertheless, due to the tenacious efforts of growers, vines continued to be cultivated and grapes harvested. Rheims was three quarters besieged all through the war, and even occupied for a short time (4 to 13 September, 1914). Only 1,500 meters separated the front line and the town, 90 % of which was destroyed by continual bombardment.

Mumm's cellars, like those of other champagne Houses, were partially occupied by French troops defending Rheims: as of 1915, they sheltered the officers of an entire division. They were also used for civilian purposes; an academic group, called the Joffre school, studied there. A chapel was built on the request of Cardinal Luçon, archbishop of Rheims, and its consecration followed by a light meal at the house of Georges Robinet: the untimely arrival of a shell however deprived the cardinal of his reviving cup of chocolate.

The storerooms were in ruins, so all work was done in the cellars, where women took over the tasks of *remuage* and *dégorgement.* Enough champagne was produced to allow Mumm to break even under these difficult conditions — 1,700,000 bottles in 1914, a year of partial peace, and a total of 1,000,000 bottles over the remaining war years. Quality was very good because this grim period produced one of the best vintages of the 20th century (1914), and two other excellent ones (1915 and 1917).

The wine however, had to reach consumers, and champagne came well down the list of transport priorities. Wine was sent by dangerous and uncertain routes with limited traffic, to either Dormans (rail from Rheims) or Epernay (road to Rilly-la-Montagne, then rail), both of which connected with the Paris-Nancy line.

△ *School in the cellars,*
in 1916.

Sales continued, despite transport problems, and increased prices due to production difficulties and high freight costs. Exports to the United States and Canada went downhill rapidly because of the Atlantic war and, above all, prohibition. Sales to countries at war with France ceased entirely, followed not long after by Russia. Demand elsewhere remained strong, especially in France and Great Britain, since champagne was doing its bit for the war effort. The government decided in 1917, when the morale of the French army was at its lowest ebb and some units were starting to mutiny, to give a bottle of champagne to every serviceman on New Year's Day, 1918: Mumm was among those suppliers charged with provoking euphoria in the regiments. In 1918, at the time of the German onslaught, a colonial division was stationed in Rheims, and promised two bottles of champagne per man per day, for protecting the town......they stayed on to the bitter end. Champagne was also the best aviation fuel: in French and British airmen's messes, war trophies were replaced by wall-trophies made out of champagne corks. The wounded, and soldiers on leave, were revived with champagne. In the British army, according to the *Vigneron Champenois* of 21 October, 1914, *there were 150 tins of condensed milk and 10 bottles of champagne allocated in field first-aid chests for everytime 1,000 men.* The press spoke of the "godsons of war," who swigged the wine of hope with their war girlfriends.

Although Mumm had no difficulty finding willing paying customers, soldiers sheltered in the cellars drank up free of charge. Bottles were not affected by the hostilities, but nevertheless disappeared mysteriously — though in moderate quantities. It was discovered one day that the full cases used as seats for religious functions had become empty cases. Reserve wines were also lost because soldiers filled their hip flasks from the big famous Palatinate casks.

The German offensive threatened Rheims in the Spring of 1918, and on 25 March the authorities ordered the town to be evacuated. Mumm, like other champagne Houses, was authorised to retain a skeleton staff only, who were fed by the army still occupying the cellars. Production ceased until better days.

On 11 November, 1918, the armistice was finally signed, and peace reigned once more. Around Rheims, *in November 1918, were nothing but ruins; there were no more dwellings or storerooms, parts of the cellars were flooded, and equipment was scattered about or had disappeared.* Stocks were still considerable, despite the pillaging which had taken place, but some wines had spoiled due to lack of attention, and some had been destroyed in the storerooms or during transport. The loss to the champagne trade was evaluated at seventy-two million francs — twenty million for buildings, an equivalent amount for the aggregate of wine, goods, tools and equipment, and the difference for bad debts incurred in enemy countries and Russia. Mumm suffered its fair share of all these calamities and, still being under sequestration, was in an even more precarious position.

On 28 July, 1920, the assets and trade mark of the company were publicly auctioned by the State, and purchased by the firm of Optorg on behalf of a company formed on 4 August, called "Société Vinicole de Champagne Successeur de G.H. Mumm and Co." for 85 million francs. Its registered offices were in Paris, at 63 Avenue des Champs-Elysées, its registered estate in Rheims, at 29 rue du Champ-de-Mars. The board of directors consisted mostly of industrialists from the Paris and the North, with Jules Lorthiois as chairman, followed by James Schwob d'Héricourt on his death in 1928.

This barely established company had to face threatening competition from its German rivals. The Mumm family, henceforth living in Germany, had decided not to abandon a business it knew how to run profitably. Unable to take over the Rheims establishment again, it founded a company in 1920 under the collective name of "G.H. Mumm and Co." in Berne. The beneficiaries of Mumm unhesitatingly put a red stamp on the labels of their *cuvée* in order to mimic Cordon Rouge. In 1932, they even contemplated founding a champagne business in Epernay called "G.H. Mumm and Co."

French-German legal processes designed to resolve commercial problems resulting from the war acted in defence of Mumm partners, giving them the right to put "Champagne Mumm," or any other analogous description, on all wine labels from the day after armistice. However, it took a long court battle, lasting till 1933, before the use of the name "Mumm" was finally prohibited on bottles of sekt, unless it was qualified by "von Schwarzenstein" (title of nobility granted to the Mumm family on 31 March 1873 by William I) and the date and place of the company's foundation. The new company's struggle to protect its rights against the Mumm family was not limited to Europe: it successfully sued a United States company founded by Walther de Mumm to sell wine under the Mumm and Cordon Rouge labels.

Between the wars, two individuals — Georges Robinet and René Lalou — had a profound influence on Mumm's fate.

Georges Robinet (1869-1953) belonged to an old Champagne family. His father, Edouard Robinet, was a distinguished oenologist, responsible for, among other works, the *General Handbook of Wine - The Making of Sparkling Wines* published in 1877. At the beginning of the 20th century, the Tsar summoned him to reconstruct viticultural properties in Crimea which had been devastated by phylloxera. Georges Robinet received excellent training at the firm of Desbordes in Avize, grape and wine suppliers in 1827 to M. Heuser. As sales manager of G.H. Mumm and Co. from 1904, he effectively took command of the firm during the war. The Société Vinicole de Champagne then hired him as general manager and deputy director, a position he held till September, 1940. He was an exceptional man whose competence was universally acknowledged, a boss who was demanding, but who cared for his workers and was well-liked. In 1920, he undertook to put the company back on its feet. It was then in a very shaky condition, due to war damage of all kinds plus the halt in production. The beginnings of the Depression made his task even more difficult, but he overcame all obstacles, and in a few short years had restored it to its former glory. Vineyards and production facilities were overhauled, workers reinstated, and lodgings for their families and schools for their children organised. As a first-rate taster, Georges Robinet was able to rediscover the elements which gave Mumm champagne its individual character. When the *cuvée* had to be blended, he shut himself away for a whole week and refused to see anyone, even family. The blends he put together on paper, using samples and tasting notes, were the quality guarantee for several hundreds of thousands of bottles.

René Lalou (1877-1973) was a lawyer in the Paris court of appeal; there was nothing which predestined him for his eventual career. In 1904 he married the daughter of Marius Dubonnet, wine and spirit merchant and son of Joseph Dubonnet, creator of "Quinquina Dubonnet," the famous aperitif wine. Two of his brothers-in-law preferred sport and pleasure to business but the third, Emile, who got on particularly well with René Lalou, left him to look after the running of the company. Marius Dubonnet, chairman of Dubonnet at the time, was succeeded by his son Emile. On his death, René Lalou fulfilled the role of chairman from 1950 to 1957.

He was called up in 1914 and drafted to the commissariat where, as a military under-steward, he was given overall charge of army wine purchases.

In this capacity, he was responsible for buying the champagne used for reviving the morale of disgruntled troops in 1917. He made his way to Champagne where he met Georges Robinet. These two men, whose lives would later be linked by a solid and enduring friendship, talked of post-war plans: thus the rough outline of the management team of the future Société Vinicole de Champagne was formed. In 1920, Emile Dubonnet and his brother-in-law became board directors at Mumm. Georges Robinet in Rheims was the lynchpin of the firm, while René Lalou fixed development policy and ensured its financial base in Paris. He became its vice-chairman in 1929 and chairman on 25 November, 1939.

René Lalou immediately showed he had a lot in common with great industrialists. He was a good, upright man — hardworking, intelligent and energetic. As well as an excellent businessman, he was also an enlightened art lover: after the war he associated Mumm with one of the great painters of his time.

This type of management created the favourable conditions Mumm needed to wipe out the war damage (just about over in 1926) and to get back to normal trading which had been compromised for almost seven years.

Ensuring grape supplies was top priority. As mentioned previously, Mumm owned close to 50 hectares of vineyards in 1914, principally in the Côte des Blancs. Being concentrated south of the Marne meant they were sheltered during the war. Vineyards however had to be totally reconstructed because phylloxera had progressively wrought its devastation from the 1890's. The carbon sulphide employed to combat the dreaded plant-louse had failed to halt its inexorable progress. At the end of the century therefore, the decision was taken to begin the "reconstitution" of Champagne vineyards using vines grafted onto phylloxera-resistant American rootstocks.

△ *Georges Robinet*
in his office in Rheims.

Advantage was taken of this situation to plant vines "in straight lines," leaving a passage large enough to allow draught animals to work between the rows. Instead of the forest of vine-trunks and stakes characteristic of vines grown *en foule,* a well-ordered formation of vines should have sprung up, giving growers reason to boast the best-kept vineyards in the world.

But the huge and onerous work of reconstruction was far from being finished when war broke out. In 1922 therefore, Mumm vineyards had to be almost totally restored. Workers undertook the task with courage and obstinacy: they had to pull up and replant, as well as widen paths or straighten up tracks to allow ploughs and other horse-drawn contraptions to pass through. They had to be taught how to graft, prune and train the vines onto wire trellises. The results were spectacular and, before the end of the thirties, Mumm had some of the best reconstituted vineyards in Champagne.

It decided to expand its holdings around that time, buying 11 hectares in Bouzy and 14 hectares in Ambonnay on the south-east face of the Montagne de Reims, and 8 hectares in Ay, in the Vallée de la Marne, between 1926 and 1940. These three communes all had *grand cru* status, a term designating the best localities in Champagne. A "vineyard ranking" system, set up by interprofessional agreement, operated from 1920, and permitted buying prices to be modified according to grape origin. At the top end, there were 11 *grands crus* also called *crus à 100 %* because their grapes cost 100 % of the base price fixed for any harvest. The percentage assigned to other vineyards diminished in proportion to their respective value, down to 50 % of the quoted price: these guidelines remained unchanged until 1945. Mumm completed its viticultural domaine with the purchase of 13 hectares at Avenay, and 4 hectares at Trépail, two very fine vineyards in the Montagne de Reims, bringing the total to 92 hectares on the eve of World War II. The company had thus doubled the area of its vineyards, while making sure its holdings remained in top localities, and striking a balance between the Côte des Blancs (37 hectares of former purchases), and black grape vineyards (55 hectares, of which 42 were recent acquisitions) — a remarkable feat.

Grapes from Mumm's own vineyards were supplemented by those of brokers and growers, to whom the company was loyally attached. Their vines were also in top-ranking localities, supplying 87 % of Mumm's needs in 1920, and 70 % in 1940, due to vineyard purchases. All grapes were pressed together in Mumm's press-houses, the same ones used in 1914, some of which still exist today.

Managers were responsible for all viticultural operations, at harvest time and throughout the year; M. Crochet for the the Côte des Blancs vineyards, M. Roger for those of Ay and Avenay and, from 1928, M. Vesselle for those of the rest of the Montagne de Reims.

From 1927 to 1935, French legislation set out regulations governing *appellation d'origine contrôlée Champagne* (guarantee of origin of Champagne wine). A viticulturally defined "Champagne" zone, embracing the vineyard communes of the Marne, Aisne and Aube was established and, in each commune, a defined "zone of production." At the same time the notion of grape varieties was given legal acknowledgement; the only black grapes permitted for champagne were Pinot Noir and Pinot Meunier, the only white grapes, Chardonnay.

Cultivation methods were specified as well: width between rows planted was set at 1.5 meters maximum, and distance between vines in any row from 90 centimeters to 1.5 meters. Four pruning methods were authorised, defined in minute detail; short pruning gave bunches optimum exposure to sunshine while limiting production, therefore ensuring maximum quality. Lancing and irrigation of vines were forbidden because they compromised quality.

A minimum alcoholic strength was decided for each vintage in order to ensure wines were well-structured, and a minimum yield per hectare fixed, both designed to discourage overproduction. At the time of pressing, the "champagne" appellation only applied to one hectolitre of must per 150 kilograms of grapes harvested; the surplus, called the *rebêche*, had to be distilled into spirits or brandy, used to make vinegar or served for everyday consumption as *vin de rebêche*.

In reconstitution of its vineyards, and methods of cultivation and pressing, Mumm always implemented the latest viticultural techniques available. Mechanised farming began to take over, more efficient products were available to fight vine pests and diseases, sprayers improved, and could be tractor-drawn or carried on pack-saddles, as well as on mens' backs. As grafted rootstocks and grape varieties adapted to the soil and vineyards flourished, the average yield climbed from a 19th century average of 20 to 25 hectolitres per hectare, to 39. Yields, which were voluntarily kept down to maintain high quality, remained low compared with some other wine producing regions. Harvest volume continued to be irregular however; in 1930, for example, it was only one third that of the preceding year.

With its champagne making equipment back in working order, Mumm was able to take advantage of post-war technical advances as they became available, discoveries which turned out to have far-reaching implications. Henceforth, vinification could be systematically controlled from beginning to end using Champagne yeast cultures which complemented the action of natural yeasts; thus every bit of sugar was transformed into alcohol. The exact quantity of sugar necessary for secondary fermentation was now

known, and yeasts active at low temperatures available, so the success of secondary fermentation was assured.

Apart from this considerable progress, little else was discovered between 1920 and 1939. Mumm began to use "agglomerated corks," made up mostly of fragments of cork stuck together, with the *miroir*, or end piece in contact with the wine, being a round slice of top quality cork, generally two or three layers thick. These expensive corks, wax-dipped to ease removal, practically did away with any "corky tastes."

Muzzles, with an eyelet added, were now placed on corks in advance, and *liqueur d'expédition* no longer included all sorts of aromatic products. Sweeter wines were henceforth labelled as *demi-sec,* or *doux,* for the very sweetest. In 1924 Mumm released *demi-sec* and *doux* versions of Carte Blanche, as well as a Double Cordon (red and green) *sec,* and *sec* and *demi-sec* varieties of Cordon Vert. Double Cordon sometimes had "American style" added to the label or back label.

Brut champagnes temporarily disappeared from the British and American markets. Cordon Rouge and Extra Dry, sometimes labelled "English Style," were the stars: they accounted for the major share of production, even though, in 1939, over 50 % of champagne was sweet. Cordon Rouge labels generally had *très sec* added, even for Anglo-Saxon markets.

Crémant was Mumm's speciality, even if it only represented a tiny fraction of its production. There were two categories — Crémant de Cramant, a *Blanc de Blancs* made from selected grapes of Cramant, and Champagne Crémant, or Grand Crémant, whose label specified its origin: Ay, Avize, Bouzy, Cramant, Epernay, Mailly, Mareuil, Mesnil, Monts-Chénevaux, Oger, Trépail. *Crémant*, a semi-sparkling champagne available from 1922, was sold quite cheaply considering it was relatively rare. It was

△ *Remuage.*

offered to a selected clientele, hence its reputation as a company directors' champagne. It was released in 1920, 1921, 1923, 1926, 1928, 1929, 1932, 1933, 1934 and 1937. The 1920, 1921, 1923, 1926, 1928, 1929 and 1934 were considered the best, a *cuvée spéciale* of the 1923 even being made. Large pre-war wine stocks meant Mumm was selling 1911, 1913 and 1914 champagnes in 1922 and even later.

Labels generally kept up with changing fashion, but a few exceptionally beautiful 19th century labels were recycled. The splendid blue and gold design of Crémant Sillery Cabinet of 1884, for example, was reissued in 1921 under another name. The post-war title, Société Vinicole de Champagne-Successeur, from October 1920 to 1924, tended to clutter up labels of that era. "De Bary" was dropped, but the eagle stayed.

Now that production was back in full swing, Mumm really concentrated on selling its champagne to restore the company's pre-war prestige. At the beginning of the twenties however, business went through a difficult period. The world economy generally was depressed, but wine, and therefore champagne, had extra problems to cope with. Increased taxes and customs duties meant champagne price rises of the order of 60, 100 and even 200 %, made all the more frustrating by the fact that other sparkling wines were taxed much less heavily. Markets like Russia, and, at the lowest point Germany and Austria, were lost. Some young nations with devalued currencies firmly discouraged luxury products; Poland, for example, tripled its border charges in 1920.

More prosperous nations, like the Scandinavian countries and the United States, were giving in to pressure from anti-alcohol leagues for restriction and prohibition of alcoholic beverages, and raising import barriers. These societies of so-called "temperants," which had appeared during the war, or in some cases in the middle of the 19th century, ended up persuading governments to legislate partial prohibition of alcoholic beverages in Canada, where seven provinces out of nine adopted "dry conditions," and total prohibition in the United States from 1919, under the "Volstead Act."

These anti-alcoholic laws were constantly violated and had devastating effects — certainly on the wine trade, but also on the morality, and even health, of citizens in those countries. Since champagne was authorised in the United States *for reasons of worship and medicinal, pharmaceutical and scientific uses*, a considerable number of people suddenly discovered some sort of ailment, and managed to get their champagne supplies by prescription. Still, this was not enough to keep imports flowing, and more serious things were yet to come. "Bootleggers" worked hard at supplying poor quality imitation champagne to the market, but brought authentic champagne into the United States and Canada as well, via Saint-Pierre and Miquelon, the Bahamas, Bermuda and Mexico. Annual statistics mentioned "probable contraband," giving estimates in 1923 and 1926.

Because its contraband price was prohibitive, only very small quantities of champagne could have been present in North America; it continued nevertheless to be part of society life. Norway was the first to repeal prohibition in 1926, other countries following suit until 1933-34, when it finally ended in the United States.

Mumm had the special problem, after a war where Germany was the enemy, of making its French identity known. Georges Robinet took up the challenge wholeheartedly. He gave priority to Cordon Rouge, a completely French-sounding name, in preference to the name Mumm at a time when people were, with good reason, sensitive about Germany. On his numerous trips to Paris he called on the great restaurants to convince them that champagne Mumm was not German wine. Lithographs made up for decorating menus bore the inscription "G.H. Mumm and Co — A French Company," other documents "G.H. Mumm and Co. — Property of the Société Vinicole de Champagne (exclusively French)." Georges Robinet published "news items" as well in the important newspapers. In the *New York Herald* of the 9 November, 1922, it was reported that *the members of the Carlton Club wanted to show their sympathy for France and validate their reputation as epicureans by serving a truly French product, Cordon Rouge from G.H. Mumm and Co., property of the Société Vinicole de Champagne,100 % French-owned.* "Exclusively French" was added to Société Vinicole de Champagne on the programme of the1922 Légion d'honneur Ball. Soon no doubt existed and, in 1924, Marshall Pétain himself attended a reception in Mumm's honour at the Nantes National Exhibition.

At the beginning of the twenties therefore, trading got back to normal. In 1922, only 830,000 bottles were shipped, compared with three million before the war; by 1924 however, this had risen to two million. Sales slowed down in 1928 to 1,300,000 bottles, because wholesalers and retailers had replenished stocks. The Great Depression of 1929 then set in, resulting in a 40 % drop in international trade. New legislation in France attacked external signs of wealth and luxury products were taxed heavily: 4 francs of every bottle of Mumm sold at 30 francs retail was government revenue, which rose to 16 francs per bottle if ordered in a restaurant after ten o'clock at night! In 1930, sales slid back once more to 1,150,000 bottles, 850,000 exported. Recovery came at long last in 1934: the following year, the one million bottle level was overtaken once again. On the eve of the war, Mumm was shipping more than a million and a half bottles annually, two-thirds abroad.

With the threat of war existing, Mumm derived comfort from the booming French market, which accounted for almost one third of sales in 1926, compared to one quarter in 1922; between 1930 and 1936 it had risen 50 % in absolute value, and in 1937 exceeded 450,000 bottles. The Roaring Twenties *(Années folles)* was champagne's finest hour. Its faithful rediscovered it and new followers came in droves: "stars," great sporting figures.....plus war profiteers and other nouveau riche for whom it was a symbol of success. Mumm champagne was everywhere — on the Riviera, in Paris — especially in Montmartre where new luxury cabarets were being frequented by the famous *courtisanes*. Raymond Dufour, the new Paris agent, asked the owner of l'Abbaye de Thélème to serve the ladies Mumm with his compliments. He complied graciously, but la Belle Otéro replied: "No, thank you! Our lovers keep us well supplied with champagne." On 20 December, 1927, the inauguration of the Coupole took place, with champagne Mumm poured into the glasses of Matisse, Bracque, Derain, Picabia, Foujita, Gromaire, Goerg, Despiau, Maillol etc. They drank so much that Raymond Dufour had to take a taxi to his office in rue de la Paix to replenish supplies, even though he had calculated a generous allowance per head.

In the Roaring Twenties, Cordon Rouge was regarded as the last word in champagne. It had its devotees, such as Justice Frinjis, treasurer of the Radical-Socialist party and president of the Club des Cents, the industrialist Arman Esders, nicknamed "The Penguin" because he always wore a white waistcoat, Pierre Benoît, a frequent visitor to Mumm's offices on the Champs-Elysées, the poet Paul-Louis Toulet, Paul Morand and Maurice Chevalier. Curnonsky, elected "Prince of Gastronomes" by his peers in 1927, celebrated his new title with an exquisite lunch for two hundred guests at the Moulin de Bécherel, and of the seven wines served, the only cham-

△ *Uncle Sam drinking Cordon Rouge*
(drawing by Willette).

pagne was Mumm Cordon Rouge. A dinner given at Voisin in 1929, by a Chilean diplomat leaving France, was designed to offer his friends, in his words, *all that a man could offer to other men.* The menu: *Chicken soup, Lobster tarts in brioche pastry, truffles in champagne, Terrine "Voisin" in port wine jelly, Tomato sorbet, Cheese, Iced chestnut purée.* The wines : *Sherry Solera 1847 — Pouilly 1911 in magnum — Chambertin 1906 in magnum — Mumm 1923 in magnum.* The only champagne judged worthy of following Chambertin was Cordon Rouge.

Champagne Mumm was, of course, at all official celebrations. When the Lord Mayor of London came to Rheims at the invitation of the Champagne Trade Association, requesting to be served only pre-1914 champagne, Georges Robinet donated a Verzenay 1906. In 1931, at the opening dinner of the Colonial Exhibition of Paris, chaired by Marshall Lyautey, Mumm once again provided the champagne, as well as sponsoring a gala evening where Cordon Rouge was generously poured. Between the two wars, sumptuous evenings reminiscent of the splendid days of the Belle Epoque were held once more, and oceans of champagne, much of it Mumm, added sparkle to the Bals des Petits Lits Blancs, the ostentatious receptions given by Princess Murat, the Duchess of Doudeauville and the Marquis of Cuevas; this was the swan song of the latter's pink marble palace on avenue du Bois Boni de Castellane.

The champagne faithful also existed abroad, despite the limitations already described. The House of Mumm, purveyors to His Majesty George V, exported a little less than 160,000 bottles to the U.K. in 1922, compared with 250,000 before the war: the same applied to Belgium.

The situation was much more serious in North America, because of prohibition. In 1920, Canada imported only 11,000 bottles of Mumm! Sales figures recovered, with 400,000 bottles sold there in 1929 but, by 1932, due to the Depression, figures had fallen to below 16,000 bottles. The twenties were a catastrophe as far as the United States was concerned: the market shrank from over one million bottles per year before the war to 11,600 bottles in 1922 and, by 1928, to 120 — at least officially. Fortunately, the situation improved in the thirties. In 1934, Mumm sold 210,000 bottles to the U.S. and established a New York subsidiary, "G.H. Mumm Champagne (Société Vinicole de Champagne, Successors) and Associates, Incorporated," with offices in the Rockfeller Center. Sales continued to rise, reaching 364,000 bottles in 1937.

Mumm's export figures for other countries were generally misleading in the twenties, especially in Argentina's case, but a few markets performed consistently, like Indochina, averaging 50,000 bottles annually. This situation didn't crush the company's spirit by the way; it even appointed an agent for Azerbaïdjan!

Competition was tough everywhere, but two champagne Houses did agree to share the Bermuda market, a particularly critical one for the champagne trade, since it was one of the bases for contraband to North America at the time. In 1924, Georges Robinet and Jean-Charles Heidsieck, chairman of Charles Heidsieck, visited local wine merchants and, as only two were possible contenders as agents, drew lots to decide!

Foreign markets improved noticeably overall in 1936 and 1937, total annual exports reaching 1,200,000 bottles. The outlook was promising, even though there was a slight downturn in 1938 to a little under a million bottles. The approaching war however, would throw everything into upheaval.

France was at war from 3 September, 1939. Champagne encountered the same production problems as in World War I, the one big difference being

▷ *A vineyard
near Bouzy.*

that the Champagne region, except for short battles which took place in 1940 and 1944, was no longer a theatre of war. This time, company vineyards and storerooms were preserved but, for four long years, the region was occupied by Germans and, if its assets survived virtually intact, many of its men were a long way away — in prison camps, doing compulsory work on the other side of the Rhine, with the Free French or the French army in North Africa. Getting vineyard work done was difficult because of the chronic scarcity of labour, products for treating vines and fertiliser. There was no manpower for the harvest and, even if workers were found, there was nothing to feed them with. Winemaking products were also difficult to find.

Mumm found itself in a unique situation because, for almost four years, it reverted to being German — and in the hands of the Mumm family! In May, 1940, the exodus of the inhabitants of Rheims ahead of the German invasion brought champagne production to a halt. Many were absent only a short time: Georges Robinet started up business again and did vintage. From the start of the Occupation, he was blacklisted by the Germans for having sheltered British units on their way to the front in his storerooms. They refused to relent and allow him to take advantage of his position as Swedish Vice-Consul in Rheims in an effort to recover the cellars of the company, occupied by German troops following the armistice. In the meantime, Godefroy Hermann de Mumm, having had himself appointed deputy of the Société Vinicole de Champagne, presented himself on 27 October in Paris to chairman Lalou, and revoked the contract he had signed on 22 October giving him practically total power in the company, saying: "You have nothing more to do here, there is no longer a chairman, nor a general manager. This is my home." In order to have a completely free hand, G.H. de Mumm offered to buy the remaining shareholders and directors out. René

Lalou refused and, on 31 October, he was barred from entering the Paris headquarters. That same day, G.H. de Mumm made his way to Rheims, summoned Georges Robinet and told him to leave on the spot. The latter retired to Paris.

Godefroy Hermann de Mumm, born in Rheims in 1908, was the son of Georges Hermann, chairman and general manager of G.H. Mumm and Co. in 1914, and Georges Robinet's trusted friend. If his attitude towards company management was, to say the least, deplorable, he was remembered as a capable boss who cared about his workers. He opened a vacation centre for the staff's children in the press house at Verzenay, and organised a canteen for staff obliged to work partly at night because of electricity cuts during the day. Most importantly, he managed to liberate almost all company workers imprisoned in Germany, and limit the number sent there under the compulsory work scheme to 15.

At the beginning of the war, the Société Vinicole de Champagne and Mumm interests reached a settlement in order to save what could still be saved, especially judgements protecting Mumm champagne against German wines labelled Mumm. The latter gave up challenging legal decisions previously granted in favour of the Société Vinicole de Champagne, and accepted that correct financial protocol would determine damages for its sequestration in 1914. M. de Mumm officially became chairman and managing director. In October, 1941, he purchased property at 30 avenue Pierre-Ier-de-Serbie, Paris, in order to transfer the company there. This was a former private hotel, built at the beginning of the 1870's for Count of Montesquiou-Fezensac, husband of princess Bibesco, on a plot of land.

From 1940, the company premises were guarded by soldiers; in the entrance a notice announced it had been "requisitioned by the 2nd German

▷▷ *The harvest.*

Army." In reality, authorities feared that there would be a repeat of the pillage of 1914, resulting in general drunkenness in German units; some declared outright that it was champagne which had won the battle of the Marne! The entire champagne economy was under the thumb of a certain Otto Kloebisch, director of the Rheims office co-ordinating German supplies. Nicknamed "the Führer of Champagne" by the locals, he had such complete control of the champagne trade that not one bottle could be sold without his permission. He sometimes took part in tastings at Mumm, which was German once more: at the end of one, he left his pistol behind! M. de Mumm however, could take advantage of its special relationship with the Germans to get the necessary materials to make champagne and particularly to sell what it made.

During the war, Mumm's annual shipments varied between 1 million and 1 and a half million bottles, one-fifth being the 1934 and 1937 vintages of Cordon Rouge. The German army was "a good customer" if it could be put that way, if only because it placed orders and fixed the buying price. From 1940 to 1944 it bought 3,300,000 bottles, whose labels were overprinted with the inscription, "Wehrmacht, Purchase and Resale Forbidden." The French market was normal, booming even (370,000 bottles in 1942), but exports were suffering because of the war. The United States, the pride of Mumm's markets, received only contraband champagne; "bootleggers" got busy once more, supplying the genuine product plus imitations. Shipments to neutral countries and colonies in 1943 were limited to 50,000 bottles. The wine was from the excellent 1941 and 1943, and the exceptional 1945 vintages.

In August 1944, when Liberation was approaching, M. von Mumm, who was getting ready to depart, took leave of his senior staff in the hotel in the rue du Champ-de-Mars. He told them, in excellent French, as always:

"Gentlemen, things are going badly for Germany. I don't know what will become of me but, whatever happens, I ask you never to forget that Mumm is a great name, which deserves to have your entire staff's undivided efforts devoted to its development throughout the world." On 30 August the town was evacuated, and General Eisenhower, commander-in-chief of the Allied Forces, set up headquarters in Rheims where, on 7 May, 1945, he would sign the surrender of German military forces.

M. de Mumm left......with the firm's profits! He was taken prisoner by the English, and after the war, devoted himself to his vines in Johannesburg and "Matheus Muller" sekt which, by coincidence, was run by.....Otto Kloebisch. At the time of Liberation, Jacques Barot sat on the regional advisory board of the Resistance, while retaining up his job as cellarmaster at Mumm. He was summoned by Pierre Schneiter, the sub-prefect appointed by the provisional government, who asked him to supply wines to celebrate the arrival of American troops. Never had champagne been given with such a glad heart!

▷ *In the pressing house.*

II
THE PROMISE
OF THE FUTURE

1

Expansion

When France was liberated in 1945, the Provisional French Government, under the presidency of Général de Gaulle, decreed all decisions made during the German occupation to be null and void. Thus, legally, the takeover by the former German commissioner was reserved and the Société Vinicole de Champagne resumed management of the House of Mumm. In 1946, its name was changed to "G.H. Mumm and Co., Société Vinicole de Champagne — Successeur." Established for 99 years in 1920, the firm's existence is prolonged to 19 September, 2067. Its capital increased from 43,125,775 francs in 1946 to 182 million in 1947, 400 million in 1950 and 500 million in 1951.

For ten years the structure of the firm remained unchanged, but in 1955 major changes occur when the Canadian group, Seagram Distillers Corporation Ltd., bought a shareholding in the company. This association strengthened Mumm's international position through the renown of the Canadian firm, whose President, Samuel Bronfman, joined the Board of Directors of G.H. Mumm and Co. in 1959. This same year sees the beginnings of the "Mumm Group" with acquisition of 79 % of the capital of Perrier-Jouët champagne, founded in 1811 in Epernay. An agreement between the two firms unified the management of their vineyards and the use of buildings and equipment, as well as expenses for improvement.

In 1968, in order to increase its storage facilities, Mumm absorbed the firm of Chauvet Frères, whose buildings are adjacent to its own. In 1972, the company acquired an 84 % holding in the Rheims firm of Heidsieck et Co. Monopole. The size of this holding was increased several times, reaching 99 % in 1980. On 1 January, 1985, the two firms were legally merged. Since then, the Mumm Group comprises of G.H. Mumm and Co., and Perrier-

◁ *Traditional* remuage
in the cellars.

Jouët as well as the Corima distribution firm. In 1985, Seagram raised its interest in the Mumm group to 91 %.

In 1945, René Lalou, who resumed the post of Chairman of the Board of Directors, becomes General Manager. He faced the tasks of reorganizing the company, whose buildings and equipment were fortunately intact, renewing efforts to increase vineyard holdings, reconstituting depleted stocks and developing sales. In a short time, with the expert assistance of such associates as Jean Couvreur and Pierre Caqué, respectively Administrative Director and Marketing Director, and Jacques Barot, Cellar Master, he succeeded in harmonizing tradition and progress and bringing Mumm back to full production.

In late 1945 and early 1946, sales were stimulated by sizeable orders from the Allied Armies, mostly British and American. The Comité Interprofessionnel du Vin de Champagne (interprofessional organization representing all producers of Champagne, established in 1941 in Epernay) set up a sales agency to handle these orders. Very soon, however, it becomes necessary to limit sales in order to preserve the level of stocks, seriously depleted during the war. This situation lasted several years and deteriorated in 1952 after the small harvest of 1951.

Thereafter, stock levels improved, in time to meet the challenge of a changing market. Champagne remained the festive drink, but now was also served more often before and during meals. It is no longer reserved to the upper classes. Mumm's clientele widens and its renown grows. 1954 sees the beginning of an extraordinary period of expanding production and considerable economic growth. Sales rise six-fold in a quarter of a century, which is astonishing for a relatively high-priced product that is certainly a luxury rather than a necessity. Mumm capitalised on that by doubling its sales, to 2 million bottles in 1955.

In 1958, Marzio Snozzi, recruited in 1948 by René Lalou became Assistant General Manager, and Jean Marcandier Secretary General. In 1959, François Taittinger, of the Taittinger Champagne firm, joined the Board of Directors of G.H. Mumm and Co. In 1960, Alain de Gunzburg, son-in-law of Samuel Bronfman, also took a seat on the Board. He became Vice-President in 1961, when Marzio Snozzi joined the Board.

To assure its continued growth, the firm increased its capital several times. In 1959 it is increased to 1,500,000,000 francs, then 20 million new francs in 1960, 40 million in 1961 and 50 million in 1962.

In 1958, as for all champagne Houses, Mumm's expansion is slowed by the production limits of the Champagne vineyards and by another factor, becoming more prevalent, the winegrowers' tendency to hold back an ever greater part of the harvest. These growers, called *récoltants-manipulants* (grower-bottlers), keep all or part of their harvest to make their own Champagne. They numbered 3,000 in 1958 and were 4,500 twenty years later. By 1982, they produced one-third of all Champagne and account for half the sales on the French market.

Through the Comité Interprofessionnel du Vin de Champagne, which oversees the best possible sharing of available grapes at each harvest, contracts set up in 1959 to guarantee this distribution. The minutes of the meetings of Mumm's Board of Directors occasionally reflect justifiable regrets that the grower-bottlers, who can dispose of their grapes as they see fit, are in competition with the champagne Houses, without the same expenses or risks. The Board members also complain of the high cost of the grapes, resulting from indexing them to the average sales price of champagne, with a high coefficient of 32 to 36%, and the obligation of paying their grape growers high indemnities in low-quantity years. In addition, the champagne Houses cannot increase the size of their own vineyards, for the areas where planting is permitted are strictly limited. Fortunately, production increase in the 1960s. New plantings, authorized in 1958, continue to 1975, increasing the authorized area of Champagne to 24,250 hectares from 11,500 twenty years earlier. Since many of the vines are young, the production is high.

1970 saw the largest harvest ever in Champagne, allowing Mumm to establish comfortable reserve stocks. But at the time this immense harvest creates acute storage problems — partly resolved by renting tank barges from the port of Rouen to hold the musts. Imagine Mumm's Cellar Master, far from his underground lair, motoring along the canals toward Rheims to check on the progress of his floating cellar!

The extraordinary rise in the standard of living, both in France and abroad, continues to contribute to increase champagne sales, and in 1970 they top one hundred million bottles. Euphoria reigns in Champagne! Mumm shares a good part in the growth. Its sales rise from 3 million bottles in 1962 to 6 million in 1972, making it the leading champagne House in Rheims. For exports, Mumm is regularly in second place among all Champagne firms. In the 1960s and 1970s, exports account for 60 to 70% of sales, and its main markets are the United States, Italy, Great Britain and Belgium.

During this period, the management of the firm is changing. Samuel Bronfman, the President of Seagram, dies in 1971 and is replaced on Mumm's Board of Directors by his son, Edgar. In 1973, René Lalou dies, in his 96th year. Alain de Gunzburg succeeds him as Chairman and General Manager.

Marzio Snozzi, a Board member since 1961, becomes Vice-President, and Jean Marcandier is named Assistant General Manager.

After the extraordinary growth of 81% between 1975-1978, a new fall occurs. Nature is in part responsible. The vine suffered so much in 1978, 1980 and 1981 that in the space of four years, less than the equivalent of the 1982 harvest is brought in. In 1981, the harvest replaces only 40% of the bottles that Mumm sells. With the drop in stocks, sales had to be restricted.

△ *Tasting.*

Prices were therefore raised, but the cost of grapes doubled in 1980 compared to preceding years owing to the low-harvest indemnity of 10 francs per kilo. This puts the price at 23.50 francs for Chardonnay and Pinot Noir grapes in the best growths. To these difficulties are added the effects of the second energy crisis which in many countries is reflected by stagnating and even decreasing purchasing power. The cumulation of these factors has a damaging effect on champagne sales. Mumm, however, has better results than many of its competitors in 1979, with record sales of 8,780,000 bottles. But an ebbing is inevitable, and by 1982 its sales have dropped by 24 % compared to 1979. The euphoria of the beginning of the decade has disappeared.

During these uncertain times, the company stands firm, pursuing its long-term projects: reorganization of sales and administrative services, begun in 1978, purchase of neighbouring offices and cellars in 1979, and, as of 1980, it concentrates on the sales of its prestige bottles. The magnificent 1982 harvest replaces 150 % of bottle sales. Nature repeats itself in 1983 with a harvest assuring Mumm of a stock equivalent to four years of sales.

In 1983 the firm groups its production capacity with that of Heidsieck et Co. Monopole, while scrupulously respecting the specific character of each house's wines. In addition, Mumm further automatizes production, ready to achieve a sales volume of nearly 12 million bottles.

Also in 1983, Marzio Snozzi, at the helm of the House of Mumm for 35 years, retires as Vice-President and General Manager of the firm but remains on the Board. His duties as General Manager are taken over by Jacques Descamps, grandson by marriage of René Lalou. J. Descamps enters the firm in January, 1983, and in 1984 becomes a Board member and Vice-President and General Manager of the firm.

In the same year, G.H. Mumm and Co., in association with Joseph E. Seagram and Sons, creates in the United States the firm "Domaine Mumm Inc.," to produce a high-quality sparkling wine from grapes of the Napa Valley in California. This new venture abroad is a logical development with the limits to its grape supply in Champagne. Such diversification is common among champagne Houses and does not damage the reputation of champagne, which cannot by itself satisfy the increasing demand for sparkling wines, of which only 12 % is champagne.

In 1984 a clear increase in champagne sales begins. Mumm's volume increases by more than 20 %, and the following year by more than 13 %. In 1986, under the labels of G.H. Mumm and Co, Perrier-Jouët, and Heidsieck and Co. Monopole, 13,685,000 bottles are shipped, 4,615,000 in France and 9,070,000 abroad.

The future would have been bright indeed, had the problem of grape supply not reappeared. Vineyards affected for several years by heavy frosts during the winter of 1984-1985 which destroyed about 2,000 hectares of vines, reducing the supply of Champagne by 4 %. Measures have been taken, however, by the Comité Interprofessionnel du Vin de Champagne in order to allow producers to profit from the surplus in abundant years. In the past, the quantity of grapes exceeding the maximum harvest authorized for the year were simply left on the vine. In 1959, a first step had already been taken: a professional "Mediating Company," usually inactive, could be put into operation in years of abundance to buy surplus grapes and have them vinified by the Champagne firms, who would agree to buy such wines within three years. This company was activated for the 1975 and 1976 harvests. In 1982, it was replaced by a stock-regulating mechanism, which, in case of very abundant harvests, temporarily blocks part of the wines under the appella-

tion "Champagne," in order to maintain market balance and to compensate for a later lack of wines by replacing them on the market. Thus, when the 1985 harvest permitted the Mumm group to cover only 56 % of its bottle sales, wines unblocked from the portion of the 1983 harvest attributed to the group raised its stock replacement rate to 87 %.

Finally, mention should be made of the new plantings authorized in 1980 by the Ministry of Agriculture at the request of Champagne makers. A credit of 5,000 hectares was attributed exclusively to winegrowers to plant each year an average of 500 hectares on land under the Champagne appellation. The surface area of the Champagne vineyards in production by 1992 will thus be brought to 29,000 hectares (72,500 acres). This decision, which has had an effect since 1984, allows an increase in overall sales of champagne of 5 to 8 million bottles a year.

2
Vineyards of the Year 2000

The House of Mumm has always given the sharpest attention to its vineyards. In 1945 the vines cover 92 hectares, but the firm sought to buy more. Since permission to make new plantings is rarely accorded to Champagne houses, Mumm tries to buy vines already in production despite their high price. In the 1960s, the price becomes exorbitant, going as high as a million francs per hectare in the great growths!

In 1953, the firm bought vines in Mailly, Avenay, Bisseuil, Dizy, Billy-le-Grand and Chambrecy. At the same time, Mumm also rented 16 hectares of vines in Tauxières. In 1985, the total surface of its vineyards reached 323 hectares, of which 110 come from Heidsieck and Co. Monopole. The Mumm vineyards have become one of the largest in Champagne. It is also one of the best placed, with a 95 % rating on the scale of growths. When the vines of sister firm Perrier-Jouët are included, the total surface reaches 423 hectares.

Constant quality of grapes is assured by a continual replanting program that calls for renewal every 25 years. When a vineyard is uprooted, the land is left to rest for a year, and fresh earth is brought in. It is treated to destroy any parasites and pathogens. The process is costly, for 8,000 to 9,000 new vines per hectare must either be produced or bought, planting equipment must be purchased, and fresh earth and fertilizer must be bought and transported to the vineyards. Then there is the expense of operating the machines for the uprooting, deep plowing, disinfection and tilling. Finally, the labour used in staking the vineyards, setting out the new vines and keeping them up must be paid for. Since full production is attained only 5 to 6 years after new planting, such frequent renewal of each vineyard parcel is a heavy investment. Quality pays, but it is also expensive.

The new vines are rigorously selected within the three varieties authorized by the appellation. Thus the Mumm vineyards are composed of 10 %

Chardonnay, 58 % Pinot Noir and 32 % Meunier. Chardonnay is particularly well suited to the Côte des Blancs south of Epernay. It brings finesse, elegance and freshness. Pinot Noir gives body, persistence of taste and longevity. As for the Meunier, its characteristics resemble those of the Pinot Noir, but with less distinction and more fruitiness. In some areas, it fares better than the other two varieties.

Mumm fills an average of 30 % of its grape requirements from its own vineyards. This high percentage gives it an advantage over many of its competitors and is a valuable guarantee of stability and quality in the composition of its wines. The rest of the grapes are furnished by about 650 regular suppliers. Nearly 90 % of them have *grand cru* vineyards, with a varied geographic distribution that is excellent for the blends. Of total grapes supplementing those produced by the Mumm vineyard, 25 % come from the *grands crus* in white grapes, 50 % from the *grands crus* in black grapes and 25 % from various other growths in the department of the Marne.

To coordinate the management of its vineyard and that of its associate, Perrier-Jouët, in 1971 the firm created a viticultural department called the "Groupement Champenois d'Exploitation Viticole" (G.C.E.V.), which the following year also assumed responsibility for the vineyards of Heidsieck and Co. Monopole. But each firm receives the musts from the harvests of its own vineyards. The vines are cared for by three categories of personnel: section heads, head winegrowers, supervisors and vine workers, a work force of nearly 180 professionals. They work for the G.C.E.V. under the direction of Georges Vesselle.

Winter in Champagne is generally rather mild, spring is variable, summer hot and autumn mild. However, there is a northern and continental influence, which is mitigated by the sea air coming from the northwest and the west. The mean annual temperature is 10°C., the minimum necessary for the maturing of grapes and even for the survival of the vine. Paradoxically, this extreme limit also gives the grapes exceptional quality.

The vines are located at an altitude varying between 120 and 180 meters. The forests and woods covering the surrounding plateaux maintain adequate humidity and tend to stabilize and moderate the climate. Average annual rainfall in Champagne is 650 millimeters. This is favorable for the growth of the vine, especially since rain is evenly distributed throughout the year.

The great growths and the first growths occupy the periphery of the hills forming the Ile-de-France rim. The bedrock is cretaceous chalk, deposited during the secondary era by the sea which then occupied the present Paris Basin. It goes as deep as 200 meters. It also absorbs heat during the day, radiates it during the night and regularizes the absorption of water by the vine, which sends its roots down as far as 3 to 4 meters below ground level to find water and nourishment. It is the ideal substrata for the vines. The early 19th-century chemist Jean-Antoine Chaptal understood this when in 1814 he wrote: *In Champagne, land suitable for the vine generally lies on chalk banks; the vine prospers and grows well there.* As for the soil, it does not have the same specific importance, although it is necessary for the beginning of growth and for nourishing vegetation, in particular by holding fertilizers.

In the rest of winegrowing Champagne, the subsoil has a certain calcareous content which is often mixed in with the topsoil. These conditions are good for the vine but do not give as extraordinary results as on chalk. Its wines are useful in blends for their bouquet and fruitiness.

In Champagne the vineyards became mechanised in 1946 with the saddle tractor, invented by a young Epernay engineer, Vincent Ballu. It was pro-

duced commercially in 1952. The tractor, high off the ground, rides above one row of vines with its wheels in the space on either side between rows.

The means of combating parasites and disease also evolved. Hand-sprayers, still used in small parcels of land, were perfected. For larger areas, the helicopter arrived in the 60s to aid the straddle-tractor. The helicopter, however, has the advantage of being operational immediately after a heavy rain to prevent cryptogamic diseases, whereas the tractor runs the risk of compressing the soil and thus harming the development of the vines' root system.

Mumm remains in the forefront of vineyard research, the results of which benefit all of winegrowing Champagne. The firm was responsible for the first successful struggle against fanleaf, a formerly incurable infectious degenerative disease. In 1970, Mumm became involved in the clonal selection of Champagne vines, using scientific methods to select and develop them with the best quantity-quality yield.

The G.C.E.V. invented a laser-guided planting machine, patented in 1980 and operational the following year. In 56 hours, the machine can do the equivalent of 1,000 man-hours and assures perfect regularity in the aligning and spacing of the vines. The G.C.E.V. tests and adopts a "non-tillage" method of cultivation, replacing tilling and weeding by regular use of her-bicides. Not only does this method gain time, but it avoids the plowshare's injuring the plants and decreases the risk of chlorosis.

In 1964, Georges Vesselle introduces new harvest equipment. He per-fects a means of bringing the grapes to the presses on pallets, using light plastic cases instead of heavy wicker baskets. Such cases are today used throughout Champagne. They can be stacked, easily washed and stored, and

△ *The composition*
of Champagne soil.

since they weigh very little but contain 45 kilos, they are much easier to handle than were the baskets, which when full weighed 100 kilos.

Spring freezes are a hazard which caused 100 % destruction to Mumm's vineyards in Bouzy in 1945, 60 % in 1951 and again 100 % in 1957. As of 1950, then Vineyards Director installed a Parennin system for automatic igniting of small tar heaters that produced smoke destined to limit temperature drop by hindering heat radiation from the ground. But the results were disappointing, and the method was replaced by one using small oil heaters which warmed the air.

In 1965, 40 hectares of the Mumm vineyards were thus equipped, and Georges Vesselle devised an automatic filling and synchronized electric ignition system put into operation in 1967. At the same time, 40 more hectares were protected by water spray. This method uses the heat generated by transformation of water into ice, 80 calories per gram of water frozen. The vine, coated in ice, survives as long as it remains humid at a temperature near 0°C., and is protected from freezing. These techniques are effective but expensive, and the rise in fuel costs has meant limiting, and even abandoning the use of the small heaters.

One office in the G.C.E.V. is responsible for relations with French and foreign research centers. Its most important activities are: studies on the physiological maturity of the grape, to determine the optimum time for harvesting; geological studies are also applied on methods for growing and nourishing the vine; procedures for grafting; new technique for training the vine; and mechanical pruning. In other words, on everything that leads to improving the quality of the grapes while decreasing as much as possible the cost of producing them.

For the winegrower, whether glorious or disappointing, the harvest marks the end of his worries and the reward for his efforts. The harvest dates are set by the Comité Interprofessionnel du Vin de Champagne, and its opening date is usually about one hundred days after the full flowering of the vine. This means that the date varies between mid-September and the first days of October. Each grower, however, chooses when to begin harvesting, according to the state of his vines.

Mechanical harvesting is not authorized in Champagne. The machines in use in the 1980s damage the grapes and their juice runs prematurely. Excessive increases in potash, iron and nitrates have been observed in the must, and these are harmful to its balance. All this is contrary to the regulations of the appellation, which require conformity with "local, loyal and constant usages" and would lead to a reduction in the organoleptic qualities of the wines destined to become Champagne.

Each year the G.C.E.V. recruits an army of 1,100 harvesters to pick the grapes of the Mumm Group. Traditionally they come from the North and East of France, miners and factory workers, who arrive with wives and working-age children, parents and grandparents. It is not unusual to find 75-year-old grandmothers who have been picking grapes for more than half a century! Regularly hired by the same Champagne firm, most return every year. Their seasonal presence raises the question of their lodging. For a long time, they slept on straw, men and women in the same building. When he entered the firm, René Lalou joked that if he were to be the godfather of all the babies conceived during the harvest, his fortune would never suffice to buy them all Christmas presents! He thus began modernizing the old buildings and in 1948 put up a new building in the Briquettes vineyard, near Avize, which houses 200 harvesters in excellent comfort, hygiene — and morality!

Since harvest housing is used scarcely two weeks in the year, aside from lodging a few G.C.E.V. employees and storing vineyard equipment, the investment is large. Thus, the firm experimented with the use of tents, and now 50 % of the harvesters in the new vineyards are lodged in them. Nevertheless, the Mumm group owns a total of 12 harvest buildings scattered through the areas of the Massif de Saint-Thierry, the Montagne de Reims, the Vallée de l'Ardre, the Vallée de la Marne and the Côte des Blancs. More than 1,000 harvesters are hired each year. They are grouped into teams called *hordons* and work for ten to twelve days. They cut the bunches using pointed clippers with which they simultaneously remove unsatisfactory grapes. They are paid according to the amount of grapes they cut.

Once harvested, the grapes from the Mumm vineyards and those of their suppliers are transported gently to the seven pressing houses, each of which contains three to six presses for a total of 31. Some 200 press workers also hired for the harvest put the intact bunches into the presses. Most of these are "Champagne presses" which are also called "traditional presses" that are direct descendents of the 17th century *étiquet* presses which were largely responsible for the early success of Champagne. Only the power source has changed, since then electricity has replaced human muscle. The few presses of other types belonging to the group were modified before use so that the juice, or must, they extract is identical to that obtained by the traditional presses.

The pressing is done rapidly so that the must, destined to make white wine, will not be stained by contact with the dark skins of the black grapes. The same procedure is used for the white grapes. In this way, the undesirable substances contained in the skins, the seeds and the stems do not enter the must.

In accordance with Champagne regulations, 4,000 kilograms of grapes are put into the press. The juice that runs out is divided exactly as we saw was done in the 19th century. First come two or three pressings, for a total of no more than 2,050 liters, which constitute the *cuvée* and which will be used to make high-class champagnes. The 410 liters from the next pressings are called the "first *taille*." Lastly come 206 liters, the "second *taille*" which will be sold to producers of minor champagnes. Thus, a total of 2,666 liters is pressed, which corresponds to the authorized yield of 100 liters of juice for 150 kilograms of grapes in Champagne. The juice that continues to run from the press is called the *rebêche* and cannot be used to make champagne. Usually it is sold to distilleries.

After having been pressed from the grapes, the *cuvée* and the *tailles* remain in separate tanks corresponding to their respective categories to settle any solid matter in suspension, called the *bourbes* and deposit it out. This is called *débourbage*. Then they are transported to the Mumm cellars for vinification.

3
Of Wines and *Cuvées*

Mumm Champagne is made strictly according to the rules of *appellation d'origine contrôlée* for champagne, which guarantee the authenticity of a wine coming exclusively from Champagne and conforming to a number of specific requirements.

Regarding vinification, Mumm was among the first houses in Champagne to replace somewhat unreliable barrel fermentation with fermentation in technically controlled vats. Today the firm uses both cement vats lined with ceramic tile and stainless steel tanks. There are 780 vats in all, with purposely limited individual capacity so that each wine can be vinified separately, to retain the distinct personality of wines of various origins. The cellars are air conditioned to keep fermentation temperatures between 18 and 20° C., which best develops the organoleptic qualities of the wines by assuring the regularity of the process.

Other vats are used for reserve wines, totalling 24,000 hectoliters. The overall capacity of the Mumm vat houses is nearly 150,000 hectoliters, the equivalent of 20 million bottles.

By increasing its vineyard holdings, Mumm has been able to enlarge the range of wines which make up its blends. Each blend is a creation. On the tables of the tasting room where it is put together there are up to 150 samples, an incredibly rich range of wines, but exactly what is needed to best harmonize vinosity, freshness, elegance and aging capacity. In 1959, for example, it would have been difficult to get sparkling wines from some *crus* which attained 13% alcohol. When they were blended with less alcoholic wines, the difficulty was overcome and Mumm made a highly elegant 1959.

In the years after World War II, large sizes of Champagne bottles were introduced. In 1952, Mumm made a jeroboam and in 1953 a methuselah, followed in the 70s by the salmanazar, respectively containing 4, 8 and 12

▷ *The Mumm Museum,*
antique tools
for making Champagne.

bottles. As of 1985, the firm again produced two enormous bottles, of which a few samples had been made 30 years before, the balthazar (16 bottles) and the nebuchadnezzar (20 bottles).

In the postwar period the consumers' taste turned to less sweet wines. Thus, champagne is now much drier than it was 50 years ago. Its dosage (the addition of sweetness) varies according to the country to which it is being shipped. Per liter, the dosage varies from 6 to 10 grams for brut, from 24 to 32 grams for *sec*, and from 45 to 50 grams for *demi-sec*. Cane sugar is always used.

In 1975 automatic bottle *remuage* finally began to be used in Champagne. The aim of *remuage* is to bring all the deposit in the wine down onto the cork in order to be able to expel it. For over a century, wine firms had hoped to replace man by a machine in this process, which is long and labour intensive. A patent was already taken out in 1875 for a *"machine à remuer"* but only as of the 1970s did some mechanical means prove totally satisifactory. In 1983, Mumm made a full-scale trial of automatic *remuage* with one million bottles by *gyropalette*. In this process, the bottles remain in a container during the whole operation, which is computer-controlled. This system has numerous advantages: considerable savings in labour; the possibility of functioning under computer control 24 hours a day, 7 days a week; identical remuage of all bottles and a considerable saving in space. Manual treatment of one million bottles requires 2,000 square meters of cellar, whereas for automatic *remuage* only 400 are needed. The firm continued improving its installations in 1984, and by 1985, 80 % of its champagne bottles underwent automatic *remuage*.

Since 1945, the cellars have had to be enlarged several times. It was to gain space that in 1968 the firm bought out the adjoining firm of Chauvet

Frères, whose cellars it had been renting since 1965. This acquisition added a storage capacity of 2 million bottles. In 1975, three levels of new cellars were dug on land belonging to the firm, increasing its storage capacity by 8 million bottles. In 1979 new acquisitions increased capacity by another 5 million bottles. Most recently, in 1985, the association with Heidsieck and Co. Monopole again increased cellar storage capacity to over 35 million bottles.

The cellar galleries are dug into the chalk, on two or three levels, from 5 to 16 meters below ground level. The total length of Mumm's cellars is 19 kilometers, including 7 kilometers belonging to Heidsieck and Co. Monopole, which in 1985 were connected to the Mumm cellars by a new tunnel 100 meters long. The total surface area of these galleries is 84,000 m². The temperature of the cellars, 11 to 12°C., is constant and humidity varies from 70 to 90%. These are ideal conditions for making and aging champagne. A valuable collection contains vintage wines, some very rare, the oldest of which goes back to 1893.

In contrast to the first fermentation, which took place in large vats, it is in the intimacy of the bottle and the cool of these cellars that the blended wine undergoes a second fermentation that lasts about six weeks. Now it is champagne, and it is left to lie in absolute quiet for three to five years, aging on its lees. During this time the wine is enriched by contact with the yeasts, with reciprocal effects occurring and even continuing by autolysis after the death of the yeast cells. Such a long wait is necessary for the wine to age properly, to attain balance and to reach its full organoleptic qualities. When the bottle is disgorged, the yeasts are removed and the wine will improve no more. Its aging is ended.

Mumm sells eight wines in two ranges. The range of "Cordons" (ribbons) includes Cordon Rouge (red ribbon), vintage and non-vintage, Cor-

▷ *The laser planting machine.*
Center, in vitro *viticulture.*
▷▷ *The new cellars.*

don Rosé, Double Cordon and Cordon Vert (green ribbon); all these wines existed before World War II. In the other range are special wines such as Mumm de Cramant, successor to the former "Crémant de Cramant," and two prestige wines, René Lalou and Mumm de Mumm, launched respectively in 1969 and 1987.

Cordon Rouge has a history of over a hundred years. This *brut* champagne par excellence is a fresh, vivacious wine whose bouquet reflects the aromas of the Chardonnays and black grapes that go into it, the latter accounting for three-quarters of the *cuvée*. Over forty different wines are used in its composition, with about 20 % of reserve wines for enrichment and harmony. It can be drunk on any occasion with any dishes.

When it is vintaged, Cordon Rouge is made exclusively of the best wines of a great year. Then it finds its best place during the second half of a meal, but wine-lovers will appreciate it at any time, for the pleasure of tasting a very great wine.

With Cordon Rosé, the tradition of Mumm rosé abandoned in the 20s was reinstated in 1957 with the 1952 wine. It is a *brut* vintaged Champagne with a particularly fruity style, due to the judicious addition of a high-quality Bouzy rouge. It is sturdier than other Mumm champagnes, and in a meal it should accompany game and cheeses.

The Double Cordon is the former Extra-Dry, still widely sold under the latter name in North America. It comes from the same growths as Cordon Rouge, but receives a higher dosage of *liqueur d'expédition*. It is a *sec* and accompanies well both sweet dishes and *foie gras*. Cordon Vert, whose label is sometimes also marked "Dry" or "Rich" in English-speaking countries, is akin to Double Cordon but is sweeter. It is a *demi-sec* Champagne and the wine for dessert, pastries, and festive birthday cakes.

144

The Mumm de Cramant is a *crémant*, a *brut* champagne from the famous *grand cru* of the Côte des Blancs where Mumm has a large vineyard. Being a *crémant*, the pressure it contains is less than that in other Mumm champagnes. It is a very elegant wine, with light bubbles and surprising freshness. Its incomparable bouquet makes it one of the best *blancs de blancs*. It is an ideal apéritif, but also a fine accompaniment to shellfish and fish, in a meal where it should be followed by a Cordon Rouge.

Because of the richness and extent of its resources in grapes and reserve wines, Mumm also has a limited but regular production of two other special wines, René Lalou and Mumm de Mumm. These are vintaged Champagnes from great years, associating the body of Pinot Noir with the finesse of Chardonnay. They are made only from great growths that have undergone long aging.

The René Lalou champagne carries the name of its author, who composed it four years before his death after having guided the destiny of the House of Mumm for over half a century. The predominance of Montagne de Reims grapes in its composition gives it a solid structure. As for Mumm de Mumm, a large proportion of Pinot Noir from the Vallée de la Marne gives it a more supple, open character.

Mumm generally puts its vintaged wines on the market four to six years after the harvest of the grapes it is made from. This is longer than the requirement of the *appellation d'origine* rules, which state that a vintaged Champagne must be aged a minimum of three years before sale. Cordon Rouge 1947, 1973 and 1976 were respectively sold in 1953, 1978 and 1981. Since the War, the following wines have been vintaged (the years in italics are those of exceptionally good wines): 1945, *1947*, 1949, *1952, 1953, 1955*, 1958, *1959*, 1961, 1962, 1964, 1966, *1969*, 1971, *1973*, 1975, 1976, *1979* and

145

▷ *Vice-President Managing Director, Jacques Descamps.*
The new Mumm de Mumm cuvée.
▷▷ *Former Chairman of the Board René Lalou.*
The Rheims headquarters.

1982. To this list will be added other years, no doubt beginning with 1985.

In 1958 the painter Foujita, a friend of René Lalou and who will be mentioned again below, made him a painting of a beautiful rose. The flower, which is supposed to live only for a morning, has endured for 30 years on the collar label of Cordon Rosé. In the early 1980s the originally white foil on the neck of bottle took on the color of red gold. The appearance of Foujita's rose on the first bottles of Rosé was a real event. During a banquet at the Elysée Palace, residence of the President of France, where the Cordon Rosé was served for the first time, the wine steward was besieged and even was slipped money by influential guests who all wanted one of the empty bottles in order to have it signed by the artist.

In good years, Mumm produces a small quantity of Coteaux Champenois which are not sparkling wines and have their own *appellation d'origine contrôlée*. For the whites, they are Avize and Cramant, high-quality Chardonnay wines from Côte des Blancs *premiers crus*. For the reds, it is Bouzy, the most famous of Pinot Noir red wines, from the great growth situated on the south slopes of the Montagne de Reims. Cavoleau wrote in 1827 in this manual *Oenologie française* that *the bouquet of the red wines of Bouzy is close to that of the best growths of Burgundy*. In 1868, Jules Guyot, going one better in his *Etude des vignobles de France*, flatly declared: *The red wine of Bouzy is really one of the great wines of France*.

4

The Prestige of Champagne

It does not suffice to produce more and better wines — these wines must also be sold, and sold at the right price. We have seen the obstacles that had to be overcome in the development of Mumm's marketing efforts since the last war. Added to a difficult economic situation was ever more lively competition. This competition consists of course of other sparkling wines, whose annual production exceeds 1.5 billion bottles! But it also comes from other producers of real champagne — grower-bottlers, cooperative-bottlers (some of the largest of which produce over six million bottles a year) and a hundred other Champagne firms. There are about 8,000 brands of champagne.

In order to sell more than ten million bottles annually, Mumm must adopt an aggressive sales approach, based on realistic prices, a careful selection of markets, a modern distribution network, an effective sales force and a well-adapted promotion of its name, as will be seen later.

Champagne cannot be cheap. It can be sold for a high price simply because of its image. This was expressed in 1978 by Georges Prade, chronicler: *In order not to regress, champagne must keep its place among the desirable things of life that can only be obtained by effort, reflection and expense.* Nevertheless, the price of champagne depends mostly on what goes into it. In Champagne, the grape costs five to eight times more than in regions producing table wines, and the better the grape variety and the higher the class of the growth, the more expensive the grape. About 1.3 kilograms of grapes go into a bottle of Champagne. In the early 1980s this represented 25 to 30 francs a bottle. Added to this price is the cost of making the wine itself. Aging the wine in the producer's cellars is expensive. For most industrial products, stock is considered dead weight that must be reduced to the minimum; for Champagne, stock is the price that must be paid for quality. Keeping wines in the cellars requires large capital. This stock of wines is said

149

to be the wealth of the producer, but it is a costly wealth. Financing this "fortune" is expensive and can even become prohibitive in times of expensive credit and high interest rates. Since the bottles must be aged an average of three years, for every bottle sold the firm must have three in reserve (in addition to the usual stocks).

On the other hand the cost of Champagne is only relative, for it is the least expensive of great wines. At the end of the 18th century and the beginning of the 19th, its price was approximately the same as that of the best growths of Bordeaux and Burgundy. In 1803 a wine list from the Restaurant Véry indicates: *Champagne mousseux, 5 livres 10 sous — Champagne Sillery, 7 livres — Romanée-Saint-Vivant, 6 livres — Bordeaux-Laffitte, 7 livres.* In Christie's 1788 catalogue one found *Champagne Ay, white, 54 shillings — Château Margaux, 49 shillings.* In 1986, a Paris retailer's catalogue listed Mumm Cordon Rouge 1982 at 130 francs, but Romanée-Saint-Vivant and Château Margaux of the same year respectively at 250 and 600 francs!

The difference could be even greater in restaurants. Champagne is also ready to drink when it is bought, whereas a Médoc from Bordeaux or a Côtes de Nuits from Burgundy, for instance, should be laid down for a long time — ten to twenty years — before it is ready to drink. In fact, it appears that the price of champagne follows the retail price index, which is not the case for all wines. Lastly, it is interesting to note that in order to buy a bottle of Cordon Rouge, an unskilled worker in France had to work one week in 1900, two days in 1950 and two hours in 1980!

Mumm's gross income increases constantly, making it the second largest shipper among all Champagne firms and the largest in Rheims. It belongs to the exclusive Syndicat de Grandes Marques (union of the major brands), whose conditions for membership it more than meets: *To sell annually under*

152

MENU DU BANQUET

offert à Monsieur le Professeur Baud Le 29 Janvier 1845.

1er Service.	2e Service.
Huîtres.	Selle de Chevreuil.
Potage au Vermicelle.	Faisans rôtis.
Barbeaux à la Hollandaise.	Bécassines rôties.
Croquettes aux truffes.	Truites Saumonées au bleu.
Filet de Bœuf à la Godard.	Jambon d'Ardennes.
Chapons truffés et braisés.	Buisson de Homards.
Salmis de Bécasses.	Pâtés de foie gras.
Mayonnaise de filets de Soles.	Truffes au vin de champagne.
Punch à la Romaine.	Asperges.

Glaces.	Ananas.
Pièces montées.	Poires.
Marrons de Lyon	Dessert.

VINS.   VINS.

Sauterne.	Larose.
Coteau.	Chamberlin.
Madère.	Marcobrunner.
St Emilion.	Oporto.
St Estèphe.	Champagne mousseux.
Rosan.	Crémant.
	Mumm

Lith. de P. Barella, à Louvain.

its name at least 0.5% of total sales by Champagne firms, to have as its main activity the sale of this brand, to have a continual and traditional export activity, to sell wines that are consistent and of high quality, obtained by blending, to follow the traditions of major-brand Champagne, and to be incontestably well known.

Mumm's renown is so evident that it is associated with prestigious as well as unusual events. In May 1968, during the student unrest in France, I had occasion to go to the University in Toulouse, and on the sun-filled lawns of the campus, I listened to the students remodelling the world — but around a magnum of Cordon Rouge! And why not mention the memorable break-in at the Société Générale de Banque in Brussels on April 11, 1980. The thieves were caught in February 1981, thanks to fingerprints they left on a bottle of Mumm they drank in the vaults! Such stories illustrate Mumm's presence on local markets.

Of the 11,130,000 bottles dispatched in 1986, one-third were sold in France. The firm needs to be solidly represented on the French market because this is an important show window for its products. Nevertheless, Mumm distinguished itself by its exports, and this tradition dates from the reign of Charles X (1824-1830). The firm sells most of its production outside France, while overall, Champagne producers export only one-third of their wines. Mumm's exports follow the general tradition of the 19th century, when, in reverse of today's situation, two-thirds of Champagne production was exported. In the ranking of exporters, Mumm holds the fourth place among commercial firms of the Champagne-Ardennes region and second among all Champagne producers. Thus, its character is clearly international.

These results are all the more impressive considering the difficulties involved in exporting. Aside from Great Britain and two or three other

European countries, the clientele in foreign countries are not as easy to define or classify as in France. To make a place for oneself requires a large financial investment, much patience and the capacity to supply foreign markets regularly with high-quality wines. In addition, these markets are capricious because they are strongly influenced by both national and international economic factors. When a country's economic situation declines, one of its first measures is usually to restrict imports of luxury products, and even to stop them entirely. This was the case in Nigeria in April 1977, whereas just two years earlier this country was the leading African buyer of champagne and the tenth world-wide. Even the apparently most solid and most promising markets can thus disappear from one day to the next.

The image and flag-bearer of France, champagne is the first to suffer from international political strains. At a time when the United States was its main market, bottles of Mumm were removed from retail show-windows after General de Gaulle, during what was called the "chicken war," used terms that the Americans considered insulting. The same thing occurred in Italy in retaliation for measures taken by France to limit importation of Italian table wines.

A multitude of problems comes from the domestic regulations of each country. Thus, every bottle of Mumm sent to Abu Dhabi must have a label stating the country of origin, the quantity contained, the dates of production and packaging, the composition of the product by decreasing quantities of ingredients and, last but not least, the "sell by date!" In some countries such as Sweden and Canada state monopolies control the sale of alcoholic beverages. Not to speak of inflation and fluctuating exchange rates, which do not always work the way one might wish.

Abroad, Champagne is still considered a luxury product and taxed as

155

such, often prohibitively. Unbelievable disparities can exist in some countries such as the United States. In Minnesota, champagne has been hit by state taxes eighteen times as high as in next-door Wisconsin! Import duties in some countries reach 600% of the wholesale price of the bottle, and they are always much higher than those applied to still wines.

When these often exhorbitant taxes are added to costs of middle-men and transportation, champagne can sometimes reach astoundingly prices abroad. For Japan — and this is only one example — the price of a bottle leaving Rheims is increased 31% by import duties, 70% by consumer tax, 50% for transportation and miscellaneous costs, 22% for the agent's commission, 27% for the wholesaler's commission, and 90% for the retail margin. In all, the cost of the bottle triples. This explains the difficulty in exporting to Japan, where Mumm has nevertheless made a big effort. The main foreign markets for Mumm in the 1980s are the United States, Canada, Switzerland, Great Britain, Italy, West Germany and Belgium. These are also the main importers for all of champagne. But the firm is represented, and often well placed, in over 160 markets, and occupies an honorable place on the balance sheet of French international trade. Cordon Rouge even surged into the Chinese market in 1979, aided more than just a little by its red stripe, the symbol of happiness in the Celestial Empire.

It would take too long to detail the characteristics of every market. It suffices to note that Mumm is still highly active in North America. It is regularly the second-largest exporter to the United States, which remains its principle foreign market with over 25 million bottles sold in 1985. It is by far the largest in Canada, with a constant 40% or more of the Champagne market, and has sold more than 700,000 bottles in one year.

Mumm is purveyor to various royal courts, another tradition that, as

*Mumm Champagne
abroad in the 1950s.*

we saw, dates from the very beginnings of the firm. In Great Britain, ever since Mumm Champagne was served at the table of Queen Victoria, this privilege has been underlined by the "Royal Warrant," a seal placed on each bottle of Cordon Rouge destined for Buckingham Palace, and renewed in 1986 when "*Messrs. G.H. Mumm and Company*" were awarded "*Place and Quality of Purveyors of Champagne to Her Majesty.*"

Mumm also supplies numerous "republican courts." Ever since the early 60s, almost all the Heads of State in French-speaking Africa have served their guests bottles of Mumm with the label "Purveyor to His Exellency the President of the Republic of..." It is the same in Europe, and Mrs. Finbogadottir, President of Iceland, wrote a gracious letter about the *Cuvée* René Lalou to Mumm's agent in Iceland: "*Heartfelt thanks for kindly having sent me so special and noble a wine that one hardly dares look at it without wearing an evening gown and silver slippers.*"

5
The Image of Champagne

The commercial success of a champagne depends closely on its image, which can never be completely taken for granted. It must be continually reinforced with promotional activities to maintain consumer loyalty and to enlarge its appeal. Mumm has been dealt a strong hand in this regard. Its high quality is well known and its image is both traditional and modern. Its distinctive Cordon Rouge bottle, with its bright red band, stands out clearly in press photos and on television. Its very name is distinctive, and its attractive sound has given rise to slogans known throughout the English-speaking world, such as "Mumm's the word."

The promotional strategy of Mumm includes all forms of communication, advertising, public relations, patronage and sponsoring. Mumm sometimes uses direct advertising campaigns in the French or foreign press, with high-quality photographs accompanied by a suggestive text or slogan such as *Give spirit to the moment* or *To underline the moment*. However, the firm prefers editorial publicity, which has more reader impact. This was the case for a campaign in the mid-70s using interviews with great chefs.

Effective indirect advertising stems from the appearance of the label or the name, spontaneous or deliberate, in cultural media. We have already seen some examples, but there are many others. In contemporary literature, Simone de Beauvoir's *Les Mandarins*: *He made a sign to the maître d'hôtel who was wearing an arrogant monocle: "Two bottles of Mumm brut"*, or Maurice Denuzière's *Les Trois Chênes*, in which for the 82nd birthday of Gaston de Castel-Bajac in New Orleans, *real French Champagne Mumm*, is drunk, despite prohibition. And we already know that Cordon Rouge is a favorite of cartoonists.

In films, the appearance of the bottle is particularly effective because of the visual impact of its label, which distinguishes it immediately from other

Champagnes. In *Once upon a time in America*, from Sergio Leone, the end of prohibition is celebrated with jeroboams of Cordon Rouge.

Mumm Champagne also appears on stage. Offenbach's operetta *La Périchole* is often given with a Cordon Rouge ballet.

Mumm has long been aware of the importance of public relations. To receive journalists and other opinion makers in Champagne, the firm has a highly effective welcoming service which in the 70s received up to 100,000 visitors a year. The service was reorganized in 1986 in order to personalize the visits of a more limited number of selected guests, for whom the impressive cellars of the Rue du Champ-de-Mars are opened. In addition to its installations in Rheims, Mumm uses the annex of a historic windmill on the north slope of the Montagne de Reims, in Verzenay. Built in 1820, the mill ceased in 1901 grinding the grain harvested in the plain it overlooks. During World War I it served as camouflage for a cement observation tower. Today, visitors enjoy its view over the magnificent Montagne de Reims vineyards as they sip a glass of Mumm. Receptions are also held in a former pressing house belonging to the firm at Cramant, in the Côte des Blancs.

Any occasion is good for celebrating, or even creating an event that calls for a Champagne reception. This was the case with a Mumm Gala in the 60s that is still talked about. It was held in Switzerland, at the Palace Hotel where Marlene Dietrich and Maurice Chevalier were honored guests. The cream of the international jet set flocked into the party. Mumm flowed freely, while stewardesses from the major international airlines served exotic foods flown in from the four corners of the world.

Among its promotional activities, Mumm gives an important place to the Order of the Coteaux of Champagne. The rules of this wine society specify that it should spread knowledge of Champagne and favor its consumption. It was created in 1956, inspired by the "Costeaux," 17th century gourmets who were reputed to drink only wine *from the three coteaux of Ay, Hautvillers and Avenay*. In the course of prestigious ceremonies in Rheims, in the French provinces and abroad, prominent figures, important clients, and friends of Mumm are inducted into the Society.

The firm also supports the "Champagne Academy," a British organization founded in the 50s by twelve large champagne Houses to train "ambassadors" of Champagne to recognize the characteristics of each brand and to insure their promotion. Each year a dozen young people spend a week in Champagne where they are successively received by each of the firms. They acquire solid knowledge on the vineyard, on Champagne and on each firm. After passing an examination, they receive a diploma. Their week traditionally ends in Paris with an evening at the Lido. Once these "Old Boys" have returned to Britain, they form a group of enlightened amateurs and get together at the highly prized Champagne Academy dinners.

Hotels and restaurants receive particular attention from Mumm. For the creation of the Hilton hotel chain, Mumm was chosen to furnish the "Management's Special Reserve Champagne." New Year's Eve sees Cordon Rouge and René Lalou flowing freely in the large hotels of European ski resorts. Such examples could be multiplied.

Restaurants are excellent showcases for Champagne, and great chefs are lovers of Champagne, connoisseurs not only for their personal satisfaction but also masters in the art of marrying Champagne with their best dishes. The most famous have been interviewed:

Alain Chapel (*La Mère Charles* at Mionnay), as a good Burgundian, appreciates Cordon Rouge as a great wine, with each vintage reflecting the mood of the vine. *Accompany a vintaged wine,* he says, *with a salad of*

THE PERSON NAMED
HEREIN IS PERMITTED TO
USE THE ROYAL ARMS AND
THE STYLE "BY APPOINT-
MENT TO THE LATE KING
GEORGE VI".

Clarendon

LORD CHAMBERLAIN.

14 JUL 1952

DIEU ET MON DROIT

Master of the Household's Department.

Board of Green Cloth.

These are to Certify that by command of

The King

I have appointed

M^essrs G. H. Mumm & Company

into the place and quality of

Purveyors of Champagne

to His Majesty

To hold the said place, until this Royal Warrant
shall be withdrawn or otherwise revoked.

This Warrant is granted to

Mons. René Léopold Prince Lalou

trading under the title stated above and empowers the holder to
display the Royal Arms in connection with the Business but does
not carry the right to make use of the Arms as a flag or trade mark.

The Warrant is strictly personal to the Holder and will become
void and must be returned to The Master of the Household, in any
of the circumstances specified when it is granted.

Given under my hand and Seal this

First day of January, 1947 in the Eleventh

Year of His Majesty's Reign.

Lord Chamberlain.

freshwater crayfish or with finely cooked fish. But if you have chosen a more solid rosé, serve poularde or white meats. Or the luxury of fresh truffles cooked in Champagne. End with a sorbet, or in summertime, with fresh peaches simply peeled and served in a wide champagne glass of Cordon Rouge. A meal with Champagne should be simple and should be intended to accompany Champagne. One chooses a Burgundy or a Bordeaux after having chosen one's menu. With Champagne, it's the reverse. It's the Champagne that leads the dance.

Louis Outhier (*L'Oasis* at La Napoule) declares: *Let us imagine a Champagne dinner. As an opener, serve fresh foie gras in a crown of brioche. To stay in the same tone, serve a Mumm rosé, in the bottle decorated by Foujita, who liked to come to L'Oasis. Turbot cooked in Champagne would follow, with a vintaged Cordon Rouge, for example. Then a partridge wrapped in vine leaves, "a tender young male in your shotgun sights," the French hunter's dream. Dense and soundly structured, a René Lalou would go well with this dish.*

Gaston and Gérard Boyer (*Les Crayères*, at Rheims), being Champenois, obviously have their own ideas about the proper association of food and champagne. For them, *nothing is better than a dinner for two, accompanied by a single bottle throughout the meal.* For such a dinner, Gaston, the father, would serve *stuffed turbot followed by fresh game and a pear charlotte for dessert, all with Cordon Rouge.* Gérard, his son, suggests *foie gras, lobster à la nage, wild strawberries and a bottle of René Lalou.*

Mumm champagne is a favorite of many restaurant owners, who look for pleasure and comfort with champagne. At *Taillevent* in Paris, Jean-Claude Vrinat confides: *I arrive at the restaurant at 8 a.m. By 11, I have*

finished my preparation for the noon meal. For friends who pass by then, and to reward myself, I open a bottle of Cordon Rouge.

In Brussels, at the *Villa Lorraine,* Marcel Kreusch liked the René Lalou and made no secret of it. At Crissier, not far from Lausanne, at the *Restaurant de l'Hôtel de Ville,* Freddy Girardet prefers the Mumm de Cramant.

For René Lasserre, on the Avenue Franklin-Roosevelt in Paris, Mumm is not just for his personal pleasure, which he does not hesitate to satisfy, but every Christmas he sends his best clients a card which announces that at their next meal in his restaurant he will offer them a bottle of Cordon Rouge. Food service is an important part of air and sea travel. Mumm is well placed here, and its Champagne is available on many airlines. René Lalou was served by Air France to Pope Jean-Paul II on June 24, 1980, during a flight from Deauville to Rome. Many airlines carry their own Mumm reserve Champagne.

To create and keep up good relations with the hotel and restaurant world, Mumm frequently organizes spectacular activities for them. With Mumm as sponsor, the annual meeting of The Association des Maîtres-Cuisiniers de France, a group of the most famous French chefs, regularly becomes a tourist and gastronomic event. To mention just one, in 1982 the maîtres-cuisiniers were invited on a tour by air and sea, from Istanbul to Athens, with stops in Izmir, Rhodes, Crete and Santorini. The trip ended in style in the Greek capital with a dinner accompanied by Cordon Rouge and a memorable photo of the members, all wearing their chef's hats, on the steps of the Parthenon. Other memorable trips took the chefs to the United States and to the Baleric Islands, which Association President Emile Tingaud and master chef Paul Bocuse both say were unforgettable.

Chefs and restaurant owners are invited to Rheims as well as abroad: in 1986 in Belgium some forty of them were treated to a mini-trip on the Orient Express with the following tempting menu: *Délices de caille et foie gras frais* (quail delights and fresh *foie gras*) — *Escalope de saumon d'Ecosse à l'émincé de légumes à la vapeur de champagne braisée* (scallop of Scottish salmon with minced vegetables steamed with braised champagne) — *Vacherin au lait d'amandes et son sorbet à la framboise, coulis de framboises et fraises* (Almond milk meringue and raspberry sorbet, with purée of raspberries and strawberries).

Each year, Mumm awards its "Cordon Rouge" prize to a restaurant for its high quality-price ratio. The firm also holds an annual gala dinner for all the chefs promoted by that year's *Michelin Guide*. In 1986, it took place in the Hôtel de Paris in Monte Carlo, with Prince Albert of Monaco as guest of honour. In 1987, the dinner took place in Geneva, the city which has the highest number of Michelin-starred restaurants per inhabitant.

A large part of Mumm's promotional budget is devoted to patronage of the arts, which is inevitably well covered in the media, and it also sponsors sporting events, with the aim of developing sales by investing in the firm's image, which is essential to marketing. Such activities are usually well accepted by the public and thus more effective than direct advertising. Mumm has long cooperated with artists, although for a long time there was no question of patronage. Indeed a special relationship exists between Champagne and the plastic arts.

Painters and engravers such as Jacques Villon, Jules Chéret and Willette, have often, spontaneously or not, used the graphic image of the Cordon Rouge label. But the Champenois Willette was the first in a continuing cooperation with the art world, intended to have Cordon Rouge appear in paintings and engravings. In one of Willette's works, Cordon Rouge is represented symbolically by a seductive cupid, whose sex, like that of angels, remains in doubt. But isn't Champagne supposed to be a feminine wine? Willette decorated numerous menus for Mumm, where farandoles of scantily clad young women, in just a corset or a petticoat, or only a Belle Epoque hat, proclaim the glory of Cordon Rouge. And when it is not directly depicted by Willette, it is in the caption. In the *Courrier Français* of 24 May, 1896, one of his drawings shows a canteen maid of the Revolutionary army leaning against a cannon and, in the midst of the battle, offering a breast to a wounded hussar. The caption reads: *In those days, there wasn't yet any G.H. Mumm Cordon Rouge!*

Between 1928 and 1960, Mumm had well-known artists design its posters. One of them, by Oberlé, was an amusing composition playing on the similarity between the sash worn by the President of the French Republic and the one on the bottle of Cordon Rouge. Early in the 50s René Lalou decided to have a work painted by a major artist that would spread the image of Cordon Rouge. Through Georges Prade he placed the order with Utrillo, who chose to represent Cordon Rouge in Montmartre. A young woman of Champagne is shown wearing the famous label in front of the *Cabaret des Assassins*, rebaptized *Le Lapin Agile* after the painter A. Gil had painted a rabbit on its sign. The cabaret became the meeting place of such writers as Roland Dorgelès, Mac Orlan and Francis Carco, as well as of many painters. Seeing the woman-bottle take on enormous proportions on the canvas, Georges Prade asked Utrillo why, and received the reply: "For a Champagne magnate, one should not be stingy!" The painter refused payment and was thanked for his painting *Champagne in Montmartre* with 100 bottles of champagne.

In 1962, René Lalou had the idea of sending the year-end greetings from Mumm on cotton handkerchiefs representing works of known artists. When the news got out, many offers were received. A selection committee picked five of them: *Victoire à Longchamp* (Victory at Longchamp Racetrack) by Terechkovitch, *Jeu de verres* (Glasses) by Chapelain-Midy, *En Camargue* (In the Camargue) by Yves Brayer, *Champagne-Rêverie* (Champagne Dream) by Jean Carzou and *Champagne à table* (Champagne at Table) by Michael Huggins. Each work includes a bottle of Cordon Rouge on a table in an appropriate setting. Three thousand five hundred of the handkerchiefs were made by the Swiss firm Kreier and were so appreciated that they are now impossible to find.

The serie of pictorial works illustrating Mumm Champagne was completed in 1972 with an excellent line drawing by Trémois, entitled *Etreinte Champagne* (Champagne Embrace). The bottle does not appear, but the nude couple depicted is illuminated by the letters of the brand exploding into graphic sparks.

We have already mentioned the famous rose painted by Foujita in 1958 to decorate the label of Cordon Rosé. Since this emblem was the work of a Japanese artist living in Montparnasse, it was very logically associated with the Tokyo Olympic Games. The Cordon Rouge bottles of that period had a counter-label stating: *Tsuguharu-Léonard Foujita — Japanese of Paris — Dedicated to the 1964 Olympic Games in Tokyo — The Champagne Rose — It illustrates the Olympic wine made by G.H. Mumm in hommage to the world's athletes.* Earlier, Foujita had been inspired by the same theme to paint a beautiful *Vierge à la vigne* (Virgin with Vine) for René Lalou. He then used the theme of the rose again in a work entitled *La Petite Fille à la Rose* (Little Girl with a Rose), reproduced on a card with the following legend on the back: *This composition executed by Foujita exclusively for friends of G.H. Mumm and Co. faithfully reproduces the rose illustrating its Cordon Rosé.* In another version, the flower became a Champagne glass.

Let us stay with Foujita for an event that truly falls under patronage of the arts. Foujita was, as Utrillo, a friend of Georges Prade with whom in 1959 he was visiting the Saint-Rémi basilica in Rheims. Foujita, a Buddist, lit a candle, a gesture common to the Catholic and Buddist religions. Suddenly Foujita had a mystical illumination. Georges Prade, surprised, heard a transfigured Foujita declare "I want to be a Christian!" *Art had transformed the artist, he who had always been entranced by religious subjects, transported by the heavenward flight of the Catholic religion, subjugated by the grandeur of the Sixtine Chapel, overwhelmed by the force of Michelangelo, and left speechless before the Last Supper of Leonardo da Vinci, who touched him the most deeply for he perceived far more than the painting.* After receiving instruction in the Catholic religion by Father Daniélou, Tsuguharu Foujita was baptized, with his wife Kimiyo, in the Cathedral of Rheims on 14 October, 1959. They took the names Léonard and Marie-Ange. The godparents of Léonard were René Lalou and Mrs. François Taittinger, while those of Marie-Ange were Georges and Jeanne-Paule Prade.

In 1964, Foujita and his godfather decide to give thanks for the painter's conversion by the construction and decoration of a chapel. René Lalou purchases land on the Rue du Champ-de-Mars adjacent to Mumm's mansion, and had the sanctuary built. Foujita gives his instructions to architect Maurice Clauzier: *I want a chapel of romanesque inspiration, where my frescoes, my life's work, will remain forever linked to the essence of the Christian faith.* He follows the construction work ordered by René Lalou and then in the summer of 1966 begins the decoration of the chapel. Fresco painting is a difficult medium and physically wearing. Foujita, who has just turned 80, had never done any before. So it is a real *tour de force* that he accomplishes — for three months, from 7 a.m. to 7 p.m., he is perched atop a mobile scaffolding in a veritable balancing act. He is kept going by his faith — and by a few glasses of Mumm! He later admits that the Champagne helped him accomplish a work that went back to the techniques of the Quattrocento.

The frescoes show their Oriental inspiration, with a flowing line, and are admirably fresh and joyfully colored. They depict scenes from the Old and New Testaments. In a side chapel, *Notre-Dame des Vendanges* (Our Lady of the Grape Harvest) gives a regional note. The Virgin is seated on a cask and presents a bunch of grapes to the infant Jesus. In a background of vines appear the outlines of the Cathedral of Rheims and the Basilica of Saint-Remi.

Foujita also designs the ironwork, as well as the stained-glass windows, executed by Charles Marq, Master glassmaker in Rheims. He reproduced the deep yellow of Troyes glass, in which the sunbeams play so marvelously, incorporating it with greens and blues in a symphony of colors. The chapel is consecrated on 1 October, 1966, and dedicated to *Notre Dame de la Paix* (Our Lady of Peace) chosen in the spirit of the papal encyclical *Pacem in terris* promulgated by Pope John XXIII in 1963. It is solemnly inaugurated on 18 October and immediately turned over to the City of Rheims, which opens it to the public. People come from all over the world to admire Léonard Foujita's masterpiece.

Mumm has also been a patron of letters, creating in 1980 the Mumm Kléber Haedens Prize and in 1985 the Prize for Best Reporting. The first compensates a well-known author whose body of work reflects the values

▷ *Chapelain-Midy's*
"Victory at Longchamp."
▷▷ *Utrillo's*
"Champagne in Montmartre."
Yves Brayer's
"In the Camargue."

constantly expressed by Kléber Haedens: an epicurian concept of happiness and optimistic love of life. The winner is selected each year by four male members of the Académie française and four women writers. The Prize for Best Reporting includes two categories, reports and investigations, and columns, reviews, commentary and drawing. The intrinsic qualities of the work and the reporter's approach to the news are both taken into consideration. The jury is composed of ten journalists from the press and the radio. Since 1984, the Mumm Foundation, under the aegis of the Fondation de France, is responsible for all cultural patronage. In 1987 the Mumm Foundation presented the City of Rheims a painting purchased at auction in London, that is considered to date from the 17th century and represents the ruins of the church of Saint-Nicaise in Rheims.

Mumm has always been conscious of how much sports could enhance its image. We mentioned Mumm's participation in 1862 in the "Tir de Francfort," and in 1909 and 1910 in the Champagne Aviation Week. Today, the firm's sports sponsoring especially limits itself to international sports, whose own prestige reflects that of Mumm. In the realm of equestrian sports, the "Mumm Challenge for Gentlemen and Horsewomen" takes place in major French hippodromes. Mumm sponsors various trials, including the "Mumm Craon Challenge" which is an international steeplechase run on one of the world's most difficult courses. And not least is the 1986 French champion Mumm Pony Team of the Club Hippique de Reims. In turfing history, several horses have had the name Mumm with no connection to the firm. The Bordeaux wine shipper Eschenauer won a number of races with his horse called Mumm.

The firm also supports tennis. At the French Open, Mumm has a club at the Roland Garros courts where its tennis-playing friends are welcome at all times. As for aviation, we have already seen that Walther de Mumm participated in the Champagne Aviation Week. Thus there was a tradition to carry on, which was done in 1985 by supporting the "Bravo-Tango Cordon Rouge," a DR 400 F-GABT Robin from the Champagne aeroclub, *Les Ailes Champenoises,* when it participated in the 3rd Toulouse to Saint-Louis-du-Sénégal air rally. The plane, properly baptized with Mumm Champagne, placed honorably.

The firm has particularly close ties with nautical sports. Champagne has been linked to sailing since the 18th century when it began to be used in the launching of ships. Not without risk, for in England one time the bottle a Hanover princess aimed at the hull instead hit the head of a spectator who sued the Admiralty! In more recent times, and without incident, the foam of Mumm Champagne has bathed many a prow in marine baptisms, sometimes even consecrated by the Church.

Thus, it is not surprising that since the beginning of the century Mumm choose to be involved in nautical sports. It is the Champagne of many clubs, some of which have their own Reserve. An example is the Burnham Yacht Club in Britain. Founded in 1895, it began to stock Mumm Champagne in 1900, and since 1930 it has been the exclusive Champagne of the club.

Mumm also participates in boating events in many other ways. On 14 November, 1985, a powerboat called Champagne Mumm broke the world speed record, attaining 175.54 kilometers an hour. Mumm sponsors boat races, some of which are quite singular and do not go unnoticed by the press.

▷ *Foujita's*
"The Virgin and the Cask."
▷▷ *Foujita's fresco,*
detail.

A race is held on the Seine River, and each 7.5 meter Fun boat is skippered by a girl from the Crazy Horse Saloon, with a famous navigator as her crew!

The most important involvement of Mumm in nautical sports is in international sailing, where prestigious competitions are highly suited to enhancing its image. Of course, the winners of various races receive cases of Mumm Champagne, for instance at Nassau during the American Florida-Bahamas regatta, and at Newport in 1983 when the America's Cup was won for the first time by Australia. However, Mumm decided to sponsor a major race. In the mid-70s the firm decided to devote a large budget to establishing a link between sailing and Champagne because, according to its President Alain de Gunzburg, *adventure, dreams, and a taste for the exotic are common to both*. It was agreed that sponsoring an entire race would be preferable to backing a single boat carrying the name of Mumm. The reasoning was that the press only really speaks about a single boat when either it wins or it sinks, whereas an important world-level race guarantees wide media coverage.

The Admiral's Cup was chosen beeing considered as world championship in teams ocean racing, and its international character corresponds well to the preponderant share of Mumm's sales held by exports. The competition was started in 1957. It is open to large sailboats racing in corrected time and is held every two years at Cowes on the Isle of Wight. Some twenty nations participate. Mumm began sponsoring the race in 1977 and in 1983 signed a contract giving it exclusive sponsorship of the race for ten years, with the official name of the race changed to "Champagne Mumm Admiral's Cup." This outcome is all the more remarkable because until then the organizing committee had forbidden any advertising on the boats not more than 3 centimeters high (little more than an inch). The Champagne Mumm Admiral's Cup lasts two weeks and includes several regattas, one of which is the 30-mile

Champagne Mumm Trophy Race. It attracts large crowds to Cowes, but also to Plymouth for the gala receptions. The event is traditionally opened by a member of the British royal family.

▷ *Terechkovitch's*
"Victory at Longchamp."
▷▷ *"The Church of Saint Nicaise*
(Fondation Mumm).
Lurçat Tapestry.

Conclusion

The marine images which end this presentation of the House of Mumm naturally lead to concluding with a hearty wish of fair winds for a prosperous future. The key words of Mumm's guiding policy, consecrated by 160 years of experience and rigorous, effective work, are loyalty and quality. These are a sure basis for success at a time when authenticity and refinement in the art of living are accepted values. The myriad of golden bubbles flow which forth from prestigious bottles of Cordon Rouge, René Lalou, and Mumm de Mumm are the symbol of this success. Mumm Champagne will continue to glow brightly among the stars in the constellation of the great sparkling wines of the province of Champagne.

If one day you come to Champagne, go to the mill on the magical hill of Verzenay when summer gives way to autumn, when golden sunlight bathes the ranks of vines all around you and the black grapes are replete with promises, then perhaps you will understand the mystery of these slopes that have made the name Champagne famous all over the world.

▷ *The Kléber Haedens Prize.*
The jury and, top,
Alain de Gunzburg presenting
the 1984 prize
to Jacques Laccarière.

◁ *Princesse Anne.*
The Champagne Mumm Admiral's Cup.

Chronology

1825	1827
Coronation of Charles X in Reims.	Fondation of the company P.A. Mumm.
1876	1876
Queen Victoria is proclaimed Empress of India. Colorado become part of the United-States Invention of the telephone by Graham Bell.	Creation of Cordon Rouge.
1901	1901
Election of President T. Roosevelt in the United-States. Coronation of Edouard VII, King of England.	Expedition of 1,500,000 bouteilles to the United-States.
1909	1909
Coronation of Albert Ier, King of Belgium. Louis Blériot crosses the Channel by aeroplane.	First Aviation Week in Reims with the pilot Walter de Mumm.
1945	1946
United-Nations' Charter.	Continued rising importance of G.H. Mumm: in Italy, we will increase sales from 2,400 bottles to 400,000 bottles 20 years later.
1946	
Proclamation of the Italian Republic.	

1952	1952
Coronation of Queen Elizabeth II of England. Election of President Eisenhower.	The total volume of our sales reaches 1 450 000 bottles.
1969	1969
Election of President Nixon of the United-States. The first man on the moon (Neil Armstrong). Election of President Pompidou in France.	Launching of the *Cuvée* R. Lalou.
1976	1976
First flight to the United States of the France British Concorde, christened with Mumm champagne.	The total volume of our sales reaches 6 600 000 bouteilles.
1987	1987
15th Race Admiral's Cup: The Champagne Mumm Admirals' Cup.	Launching of the *Cuvée* Mumm de Mumm.

Glossary

Alcoholic fermentation: The transformation, by the action of yeasts, of sugar into alcohol and carbon dioxide, a spontaneous fermentation called vinification that begins after the pressing of grapes. Champagne is obtained by a second fermentation taking place in the bottle and resulting from the addition of sugar and yeasts to the still wine.

Blend: Marriage of wines from different crus and sometimes from different years.

Breakage: Explosions of bottles in the cellar caused by excessive pressure during the second fermentation.

Brut: 1) In the 19th century, a disgorged wine, with no dosage.

2) At the end of the 19th century and in the 20th, Champagne having received a minimal dosage after disgorging.

Coteaux Champenois: Still wine with this *appellation d'origine contrôlée.*

Crémant: Semi-sparkling Champagne.

Cru: Growth from a winegrowing area identified in Champagne by the name of its parish (*grands crus, premiers crus,* the scale of *crus*).

Cuvée: 1) When pressing, the first 10 barrels of must.

2) A blend of wines from many crus or growths selected after careful tasting so as to match the traditional characters, taste and flavor of a specific type of Champagne - i.e. Cordon Rouge Cuvée.

3) Once the wine processing is over, the type of Champagne obtained.

Disgorging: An operation that expels the sediment from the bottle at the end of *remuage.*

Dosage: Once the disgorging is done, introducing into the bottle a quantity of sugar corresponding to one of the various dosages used today, in increasing order: *brut, sec, demi-sec.*

Marc: 1) The load unit for the winepress, corresponding to 4,000 kilograms of grapes

2) The solid residue after pressing.

3) A brandy, *marc de Champagne*, obtained by distilling the residue, or *marc*.

Must: Grape juice extracted by pressing but not yet fermented.

Pièce (barrel): A unit of volume varying according to the different winegrowing regions. In Champagne it contains 205 liters.

Rebêche: In the pressing, the last part of the must. It is so called because to obtain it the *marc* is broken up with *bêches*, or spades, which served earlier for the *tailles*. The *rebêche* may not be used for Champagne appellation wines.

Remuage ("riddling" in California): An operation whose purpose is to accumulate the sediment on the cork by having it slide down in the bottle which has previously been tilted upside-down.

Still wine: Non-effervescent wine whose fermentation is not followed by a second fermentation as is the case for sparkling wines.

Trimming: Cutting off the extremities of vineshoots to retain sap so as to give the bunches more nourishment and with the added advantage of facilitating vine upkeep and antiparasite spraying.

Taille: 1) Pruning. Before the start of yearly growth of the vine, shortening the canes with cutters to give them a configuration that gives, after taking into account soil, climate and grape variety, the best production. Pruning is done according to the rules of the Champagne *appellation d'origine contrôlée*, which systematically favor quality over quantity.

2) During the pressing, that part of the must coming after the *cuvée*. The *première taille* (first cut) is usually distinguished from the *deuxième taille* (second cut) which follows it and both together make up les *tailles*.

Tirage: Bottling.

Tisane de Champagne: In the 18th and 19th centuries, a type of still or sparkling Champagne of very modest quality.

Vendangeoir: A building where the harvest workers are haresed and also for pressing of the grapes occurs. *Vendangeoirs* are scattered throughout the vineyards, at sites in the immediate vicinity of vines.

Vineyard "en foule": A method of cultivation used until the reconstitution of the Champagne vineyard after the phylloxera epidemic.

Vineyard "en lignes": A method of cultivation used since the reconstitution of the Champagne vineyards and characterized by planting the vines in even rows.

Bibliography

BONAL (françois), *Champagne*, Lausanne, 1984.

CAVOLEAU, *Œnologie française*, Paris, 1827.

FORBES (Patrick), *Champagne. The wine, the land and the people*, London, 1967.

JULLIEN (André), *Manuel du sommelier*, Paris, 1813.

JULLIEN (André), *Topographie de tous les vignobles connus*, Paris, 1822.

MAUMENE, *Traité théorie et pratique du travail des vins*, Paris, 1873.

PIERRE (Frère), *Traité de la culture des vignes de Champagne*, Epernay, 1931.

ROBINET (Edouard), *Manuel général des vins*, Paris, 1877.

SIMON (André), *The History of Champagne*, London, 1962.

SUTAINE (Max), *Essai sur l'histoire des vins de Champagne*, Rheims, 1845.

VIZETELLY (Henry), *Facts about champagne*, London, 1879.

Contents

Printed and bound on 7 September 1987
by Mame, Tours, France.
Publishing number : 1857. Printing number : 13398.
Printed in France.